364.1   Feinberg, Barbara
FEI   Silberdick

          Watergate

$12.90   c. 1

WATERGATE

BARBARA
SILBERDICK FEINBERG

WATERGATE

SCANDAL IN THE
WHITE HOUSE

FOREWORD BY
ELLIOT L. RICHARDSON

FRANKLIN WATTS
A TWENTIETH CENTURY
AMERICAN HISTORY BOOK
NEW YORK LONDON TORONTO
SYDNEY 1990

Library of Congress Cataloging-in-Publication Data

Feinberg, Barbara Silberdick.

Watergate : Scandal in the White House / by Barbara Silberdick.
p.   cm. — (A Twentieth century American history book)
Includes bibliographical references.
Summary: Recounts the events following the Watergate break-in
and the political scandal that resulted in the resignation
of President Nixon.
ISBN 0-531-10963-1
1. Watergate Affair, 1972–1974.   [1. Watergate Affair,
1972–1974.]   I. Title.   II. Series.
E860.F45   1990
364.1'32'0973—dc20   90-34726   CIP   AC

To my son Jeremy. In 1974, he explained to his parents that President Nixon was not going to be president anymore because he had told a lie to everybody. The Watergate crisis had even touched the conscience of a four-year-old child. I still admire and respect Jeremy's sense of honor.

CONTENTS

FOREWORD

Lest the lessons it teaches be forgotten, it is important that Watergate be remembered. This book admirably serves the purpose of making the story of Watergate accessible. Its account of the events comprising scandal in the White House is succinct, balanced, and straightforward. Although the name "Watergate" figured only in a bungled burglary, the willingness to use illegal means to serve the end of political power was the common denominator linking each of those events. It is sufficient reason for giving them a common label.

The abuses that came to a head in Watergate are traceable to three sources. The first was the deep-rooted insecurity that made Richard Nixon cynical, suspicious, and manipulative. The second was the "siege mentality" engendered in the White House by the bitter hostility toward the president's Vietnam policy. The third was the tendency toward aggrandizement of presidential power that had already been set in motion before Nixon took office. The interweaving of these strands emerges clearly in Barbara Feinberg's narrative.

The driving force behind all three was the will to win.

Richard Nixon and his close associates were uncritical believers in Vince Lombardi's axiom, "Winning isn't everything, it's the *only* thing." Coupled with the siege mentality, the will to win turned opponents into enemies. "It was all but impossible not to get caught up in the 'enemies' mentality," wrote Jeb Stuart Magruder in *An American Life: One Man's Road to Watergate.* Political opponents were the enemy. So too were the bureaucracy, the Congress, the press, and anyone else who got in the way of the White House insiders' tunnel-visioned belief in the rightness of their own patriotic motives.

To restrain this combination of organizational paranoia and self-righteous zeal would have required a firm sense of principle. In Richard Nixon the White House staffers had a boss who, instead of curbing these tendencies, reinforced them. A staffer would have needed considerable fortitude to resist the pressures generated by such an atmosphere. Richard E. Neustadt, a leading authority on the presidency, has pointed out that even under normal circumstances, "Within the White House precincts, lifted eyebrows may suffice to set an aide in motion."

Looked at from another perspective, all the abuses of Watergate can be seen as abuses of information: its theft, distortion, fabrication, misuse, misrepresentation, concealment, or suppression. Once you see it, the thread is plain. It runs from one Watergate abuse to the next. For example, the bugging of Democratic National Headquarters; the forged cable implicating the late President Kennedy in the murder of Diem; the attempt to get the CIA to subvert its intelligence-gathering function; schemes to make the public believe that the Watergate break-in was being thoroughly investigated; the presidential press secretary's announcement that all previous statements on Watergate were "inoperative"; the payment of hush money; the omission of damaging portions of tapes; the shredding and destruction of documents; the attempts to exploit executive privilege as a justification for withholding information.

But if the wrongs of Watergate were abuses of information, the actions leading to redress of those wrongs were exercises of responsibility toward the public's right to know—digging out information, leaking it, confessing it, revealing it, publishing it. The revelation of information, indeed, governed both the turning point and the denouement of Watergate. The turning point was the almost casual disclosure by presidential assistant Alexander P. Butterfield of the fact that all conversations with Nixon were tape-recorded. From there an inexorable sequence led to the denouement—the damning conversation of June 23, 1972, in which President Nixon ordered a halt to the investigation of the Watergate break-in.

Under the American system there is a constant testing of strength among the three branches of government. The remarkable vitality of this process throughout all the years since 1787 would have delighted but not surprised the men who wrote the Constitution. Starting with the aim of separating power in order to prevent tyranny, the framers set in motion a self-adjusting mechanism under which one branch checks the excesses of another or picks up initiatives avoided by another, with the interaction of the whole generally resulting in a force for moderation.

In dealing with and even drawing new strength from Watergate, our governmental system proved its basic soundness. Watergate can fairly be regarded as demonstrating the failings of men and the resiliency of a man-made institution. Its prototype was the Massachusetts Constitution of 1780, the oldest written constitution still in force. Drafted by John Adams, it declares that the separation of the powers of government is "to the end it may be a government of laws and not of men." As Adams later explained:

> [W]here the public interest governs, it is a govern-
> ment of laws, and not of men: the interest of a
> king, or of a party, is another thing—it is a private
> interest; and where private interest governs, it is a
> government of men, and not of laws.

Watergate showed us how vulnerable to the abuse of power is even our system of checks and balances. The Watergate revelations arrested a process that was beginning to substitute the interest of a president for the interest of a people. And once again, though in starker terms than ever before, we were warned that eternal vigilance is the price of liberty.

In reacting to Watergate, the Congress and the judiciary dealt with the excesses of the executive branch by asserting to the full the roles that the framers envisioned for them. The Senate subcommittee chaired by Senator Ervin went forward with public hearings on Watergate despite the concerns of the executive branch's special prosecutor, Archibald Cox. Judge John Sirica—chief judge of the district court of the District of Columbia, one among almost four hundred federal district court judges— ordered the president of the United States to comply with the subpoenas of a grand jury despite the president's strenuous insistence that to do so would subvert the separation of powers. The District of Columbia Court of Appeals and the Supreme Court both sustained Judge Sirica's order. The House Committee on the Judiciary assumed the grave responsibility of weighing charges of high crimes and misdemeanors against the president and carried out that responsibility with dignity and fairness.

On Saturday, October 20, 1973, Richard Nixon ordered the firing of Archibald Cox as the Watergate Special Prosecutor. At his press conference on that day, Professor Cox said: "Whether ours shall continue a government of laws and not of men is now for Congress to decide and, ultimately, the American people." Professor Cox was right, with a difference. It was the American people who decided, and the Congress which concurred, that ours would continue a government of laws and not of men. In protest against the Cox firing, three million Americans sent messages to Congress. Many more would have done so had they been able to get through to Western Union. No such enormous outpouring of public protest had ever before taken place. The American people could not have made plainer their determination to maintain a government of laws.

Elliot L. Richardson

A THIRD-RATE
BURGLARY ATTEMPT

In downtown Washington there is a luxurious apartment
and office complex overlooking the Potomac River, known
as the Watergate. Its many concrete balconies and curved
modernistic shape make it a most fashionable address for
those who can afford the price of an apartment or suite. In
the late 1960s and early 1970s, the complex housed many
wealthy and powerful members of the Republican party,
including important government officials in President
Richard Nixon's administration. In spite of its possibly
hostile political climate, the Democrats chose to make the
posh Watergate offices headquarters for their national
party organization. Little did the building's residents suspect that soon the name Watergate would no longer stand
for opulence and elegance but would become the symbol
of a national scandal that toppled a president and brought
disgrace to his administration.

Unlike other scandals that had tarnished the executive branch of government, the Watergate affair concerned not just greedy officials eager to accept bribes in
exchange for favors. Instead, it focused on the president
himself and the way he abused his official powers. On

Inauguration Day, each president takes an oath to "preserve, protect, and defend" the Constitution of the United States. In other words, the president promises to obey the rules limiting his authority. He also guarantees that those serving under him will obey the nation's laws. President Richard Nixon and his associates stepped outside those constitutional boundaries when they defied the laws of the land and then concealed what they had done.

The Watergate scandal was unique not only because a president was directly involved in unlawful activities. It also marked the first time in United States history that a chief executive resigned from office. It was also the first time that a president was replaced by an unelected successor. The Twenty-fifth Amendment, ratified in 1967, had provided for an appointed vice president. At that time, few Americans had expected that an unelected presidential understudy would get to play the leading role in government. However, the new constitutional process worked smoothly when Gerald Ford took over from Richard Nixon and the business of government continued.

On June 17, 1972, the Watergate complex attracted attention as the site of a failed burglary. At around two o'clock in the morning, five men dressed in business suits and wearing rubber surgical gloves were arrested during an attempt to break into the Democratic National Committee headquarters. The job had been badly bungled. The taped locks had quickly attracted the attention of building security guard Frank Wills, who summoned the police. The men were caught carrying lock picks, tear-gas guns, cameras, and electronic listening devices, called bugs. The bugs made it possible for people to eavesdrop on other people talking in a room as well as on phone conversations. The intruders had been trying to repair the faulty electronic equipment that they had already installed at the Democratic headquarters over Memorial Day weekend.

The police also discovered that the men had in their possession several thousand crisp $100 bills, with serial numbers that ran in sequence, and a notebook with the name "E. Hunt W.H." written on one of its pages. The money could be traced as could the person in the notebook. So, although the burglars gave the police false names, their efforts to conceal their identities and the immediate purpose of their mission were already compromised. The whole affair had been botched from the start.

When he was taken before the judge to be formally accused of the crime, one of the burglars, James W. McCord, Jr., identified himself as a security consultant, formerly with the Central Intelligence Agency (CIA). The CIA is responsible for gathering information on the activities of the nation's enemies abroad. The remaining four men were from Miami and had been involved in anti-Castro activities. Three of them, Bernard Barker, Virgilio Gonzalez, and Eugenio Martinez, were Cuban exiles. The fourth, Frank Sturgis, was an American soldier-of-fortune. Like McCord, all four had past CIA connections.

The next day, national newspapers ran short articles about the arrest at the Watergate complex. The incident was considered so unimportant that the *New York Times* ran the story on page 30 of its June 18th edition. While the story did not seem to deserve much media attention, news of the bungled break-in was certainly making an impression on the men in President Nixon's inner circle at the White House. For them, the Watergate arrests posed a threat, a threat to destroy the president's chances for election on November 7 to a second term of office.

The president was a solitary, private sort of man who preferred to let others deal with the people he did not want to see and cope with the paperwork he chose not to handle. So he came to depend on an inner circle of trusted advisors. Two of those members of the White House inner

circle were former advertising man H.R. "Bob" Haldeman, the president's chief of staff, and one-time Seattle
attorney John Ehrlichman, Nixon's chief domestic advisor.
As chief-of-staff, Haldeman controlled the president's
priorities—what matters came to his attention and who
got in to see him. As principal domestic policy advisor,
Ehrlichman screened problems and made suggestions
for their solutions. The two men were known as the Ger-
man Shepherds, because of their Teutonic-sounding last
names.

These aides, both graduates of the University of California at Los Angeles (UCLA), had gained political experience by working in some of Nixon's earlier campaigns.
They were part of the team that helped bring about his
1968 presidential victory and had been on his staff ever
since. Bob Haldeman was trim and tanned with a crew
haircut. Balding and stockier, John Ehrlichman had a
nervous habit of tapping a pencil during conferences. Both
men neither smoked nor drank. Yet these two puritanical
advisors were to direct some of the most corrupt and illegal
actions ever taken by government officials. In their zeal to
have the president reelected by a record-breaking margin
of victory, the president's men began to use the instruments of government for purposes the Constitution had
never anticipated.

First, Ehrlichman supervised the "Plumbers unit," located in a basement office in the White House. The Plumbers unit was a secret group of men devoted to the
president. It was set up to stop unfavorable leaks to the
news media that could embarrass Richard Nixon and
cause him to lose public support. For example, in 1971 the
group had arranged to burglarize the offices of psychiatrist
Dr. Lewis J. Fielding. They were searching for confidential
material they could use against defense analyst Daniel
Ellsberg, who was one of the doctor's patients. The Plumbers had found out that Ellsberg was responsible for releas-

ing *The Pentagon Papers* to the public. These secret documents traced the origins of U.S. involvement in the unpopular Vietnam War. They revealed how haphazardly decisions about the Vietnam War were actually made. The Nixon administration was trying to stop newspapers from publishing these potentially explosive papers. As part of its efforts, the Plumbers were trying to discredit Ellsberg. Eventually, the Supreme Court ruled that printing these documents did not violate national security, as the president had claimed.

Second, Haldeman arranged transfers of Plumbers unit members to the Committee to Reelect the President (CRP) offices located at 1701 Pennsylvania Avenue, a stone's throw from the White House. Victory was so important to Nixon that he refused to rely exclusively on the Republican party to run his campaign for a second term of office. Unlike the regular Republican organization, CRP was not concerned with the election of the party's other candidates for office. It was an independent committee whose members were personally loyal to Nixon and dedicated to his reelection. Independent committees for individual candidates are a common political phenomenon around election time. On the surface, CRP, like these other committees, prepared and circulated campaign literature, appealed for votes, and raised funds.

However, in certain offices of the CRP staff, these normal routines of fund-raising and vote-getting were jettisoned in favor of undercover operations. The men whom Haldeman, among others, placed on the CRP staff, were willing to go to any lengths to make sure the president was returned to office. Some of these men secretly collected illegal monies to fund unlawful activities directed against their Democratic opponents. Others were kept busy gathering campaign intelligence, finding out what the Democrats were planning to do, and conducting campaign sabotage, undermining the Democrats' regularly scheduled political functions and events. (In view of these activities, perhaps CREEP, as the Committee to Reelect the President gradually came to be known, was a more accurate label than CRP.)

Senior White House aide H.R. "Bob" Haldeman assigned White House counsel John Dean responsibility for campaign intelligence at CRP. This involved getting information on what the Democratic party's leadership was planning for the upcoming election. Dean had worked for Attorney General John Mitchell in the Department of Justice before Haldeman brought him over to the White House in 1970. Haldeman described Dean, a young graduate of Georgetown Law School, as "a bright, able, handsome, super-ambitious, young guy."[1]

Dean moved G. Gordon Liddy, a former FBI agent, a super-patriotic, self-styled tough guy, from the Plumbers unit in the White House to CRP. Charles Colson, another White House counsel, recommended former spy novelist E. Howard Hunt, another Plumber, to the committee. Hunt and Liddy had already supervised the ransacking of Daniel Ellsberg's psychiatrist's office. On a wall in a CRP office was a sign, "Winning in Politics Isn't Everything, It's the Only Thing."[2] For Hunt and Liddy, this was the perfect motto.

In January 1972, Liddy met with his superiors at CRP and offered them a series of proposals to conduct espionage against the Democrats. Present at the meeting were John Dean and John Mitchell. As of March 1, Mitchell was to leave his post as attorney general and become director of CRP. Mitchell vetoed Liddy's plans for kidnappings, seductions, and wiretaps, claiming that he did not approve of those kinds of activities. He also argued that they were too expensive. On March 30, two deputy directors of the CRP, Jeb Stuart Magruder, a former member of Haldeman's staff, and Frederick C. La Rue, a wealthy Southern Republican, met with John Mitchell. Together, they accepted Liddy's plan to plant listening devices at Democratic National Headquarters. They agreed to give Liddy $250,000 to carry out the operation. Hunt recruited the four Miamians and McCord to carry out the Watergate operation. This is why a number of the president's men had reason to fear the consequences when these five men were arrested for a simple, bungled break-in.

At the time of the burglary, ringleaders Liddy and Hunt had managed to avoid arrest because they had been in another section of the Watergate complex. They knew they had to report what had taken place to their superiors, but, with the exception of Ehrlichman, everyone they had to contact was away from Washington. Haldeman was with the president in Florida; Mitchell and Magruder, in California; and Dean, in the Philippines. Desperately, Liddy phoned Magruder to tell him about the arrests. Mitchell and Magruder suggested that he contact Attorney General Richard G. Kleindienst to see if he could arrange to release one of the men, James McCord, from custody. The two men were concerned that they would be compromised if the press learned that McCord worked as a security consultant for CRP. An indignant Kleindienst refused to get involved in this scheme.

The same day, June 18, senior White House aide John Ehrlichman received two urgent phone calls telling him about the notebook with Howard Hunt's name in it. Ehrlichman anxiously phoned Press Secretary Ron Ziegler to get word to Haldeman and the president. Nixon was furious. He phoned an aide, Charles Colson, who described the president's reaction to news of the bungled break-in this way:

. . . [Nixon] *thought it was the dumbest thing he had ever heard of and was just outraged over the fact that anyone even remotely connected with the campaign organization would have . . . anything to do with something like Watergate.* [3]

Winning a second term of office was to be Nixon's crowning moment, his ultimate triumph over a past checkered with defeats as well as victories. He did not want a botched-up break-in to ruin his chances. Politics consumed his whole life. It had been his road to fame and fortune.

Born in Yorba Linda, California, in 1913, Richard Milhous Nixon was raised in the small town of Whittier. His childhood was a history of hand-me-down clothes and after-school chores. His father was unable to make a go of the general store–gasoline station he owned. Working his way through Whittier College and Duke Law School, Richard Nixon was always conscious of "pinching pennies." He married Thelma "Pat" Ryan, an attractive teacher at Whittier High School. After a stint in the Navy during World War II, he returned to California to run for Congress.

During his races for the House and Senate, Nixon developed a reputation for hitting hard at his opponents in a no-holds-barred offensive. He accused them of being soft on communism whether or not the charges could hold up. He was a ruthless campaigner who wanted desperately to win. Somewhere along the line, his opponents took to labeling him Tricky Dick, coining a tag that aptly described his approach to politics. It stuck with him through much of his career. As a congressman, Nixon rose quickly in politics, gaining national attention as a crusader who doggedly pursued State Department employee Alger Hiss. Hiss was accused of communist ties, but a court tried him only for perjury (lying under oath).

Republican presidential candidate Dwight D. Eisenhower chose Nixon as his running mate in 1952 but almost dumped him from the ticket when Nixon was accused of accepting campaign funds for his personal use. Nixon salvaged his political career by going on television to give a speech explaining away the charges against him. As a result of his soul-baring references to his family and their dog Checkers, the speech is historically known as the Checkers Speech. As vice president throughout the Eisenhower years, Nixon was kept in the shadows, except when the president called on him to tour foreign countries as his representative. These trips gave Nixon expertise in dealing with heads of state and international problems. The publicity he received for his outspoken debates with Soviet leader Nikita Khrushchev and for his courage in facing an angry mob in Venezuela helped earn him the presidential nomination in 1960.

After a series of television debates in which he suffered by comparison with the handsome, smooth-tongued John F. Kennedy, Nixon met the first of his election defeats. Kennedy won the presidency by a mere 113,000 votes of the 68 million cast, by less than one percent. Then in 1962, Nixon ran against Edmund "Pat" Brown in a California gubernatorial race and was beaten by just 284,000 votes of the 5.7 million votes cast. Each race was so close that the defeats were especially bitter for the losing candidate. Right after he lost the governorship, Nixon announced his retirement from politics, telling reporters, "You won't have Nixon to kick around anymore, because, gentlemen, this is my last press conference."[4]

After five years of financial success, working for a Wall Street law firm in New York and abroad, Nixon returned to politics as a relaxed and assured senior statesman. Along the way, he had managed to shed his dubious reputation as Tricky Dick, who would do anything to win a political race. In 1968, he became the Republican party's standard bearer and defeated Democrat Hubert H. Humphrey by approximately 510,000 votes of the 62.9 million votes cast. In 1972, the president wanted to win by a wide popular margin. Such a victory would be a vote of confidence in his personal abilities, which had thus far escaped him.

This is why the president's men worked hard to prevent discovery of any link between the Watergate burglars and the CRP. The conspirators scrambled to get rid of the evidence, frantically destroying documents and memos. At CRP headquarters, Liddy hastily removed his files and other $100 bills and put them through a shredder. At the White House, Gordon Strachan, Haldeman's aide, quickly shredded other papers concerning CRP's illegal operations. Hunt rushed to his office at the Executive Office Building, took emergency funds from his safe, and hired lawyers for the burglars. As a precaution, Hunt's name was removed from the White House directory. For a while Hunt disappeared. Dean claims that he was ordered to leave the country, but then that order was canceled.

Sometime later, a worried Ehrlichman gave orders to make sure all incriminating papers were removed from Hunt's safe. The papers contained evidence of other illegal activities, such as the measures taken against Daniel Ellsberg. John Dean examined them before he turned the contents of the safe over to the FBI. He separated some potentially damaging notebooks from the rest of Hunt's documents. Eventually, Dean gave them to the cooperative L. Patrick Gray, acting director of the FBI, who kept them in his own safe. Much later they were destroyed. Gray had served as office manager of the Washington headquarters of Nixon's 1960 presidential campaign and, as a reward for his loyal service, was appointed to the top

FBI post in 1971 upon the death of Director J. Edgar Hoover. He would do his best to protect the reputation of the president and his administration.

For a brief time, it looked as if Watergate might simply fade away, to the relief of all concerned. However, an item on the Associated Press [AP] news service wire revealed that one of the burglars, James McCord, the self-admitted former CIA agent and security consultant, was actually the security coordinator for the CRP. McCord's connection with CRP was most embarrassing to the Nixon administration. The president's campaign manager, John Mitchell, issued a statement denying any connection between the break-in and CRP. On June 19, presidential press secretary Ron Ziegler described the incident as a "third-rate burglary attempt."[5] At a June 22nd press conference, President Nixon went on to reassure the public by stating, "The White House has had no involvement in this particular incident."[6] Nine days later, John Mitchell unexpectedly resigned his post and returned to private law practice in New York. At the time, few questioned his decision.

After listening to these statements, few Americans had reason to doubt that the break-in was just an isolated event. Besides, dirty politics in an election year was almost a national tradition. That is why the public tended to refer to the break-in as a caper and a prank, rather than a crime. People quickly lost interest in the failed bugging of Democratic Headquarters and directed their attention elsewhere. It seemed unlikely to them that the Republicans would have tried such a stupid scheme since President Nixon was already nineteen points ahead in the polls.[7] However, some newspaper reporters were intrigued by the fact that James McCord was employed by CRP. They felt that there might be more to the Watergate story than the administration was willing to reveal.

2

THE SLUSH FUND

Stubbornly, several newspaper reporters dug into police reports to see what else they could find out about the Watergate burglary. They felt it was foolish to dismiss the case as a minor campaign prank. For these hardened professionals, McCord's connection with CRP could not be explained as mere coincidence. There had to be more to the Watergate break-in than the burglars let on. Who had ordered a former CIA agent, now working for a presidential campaign organization, to plant listening devices in the Democratic National Committee Headquarters? Could a respectable political outfit like CRP be behind the bungled break-in? Why would they permit a dumb stunt like this to occur? The newspeople were insistent upon ferreting out the facts. The Nixon administration was just as determined to conceal the facts. Now, the press corps and the White House would find themselves locked in a contest over the control of vital information—information about the Watergate break-in.

Two of the reporters who refused to let the Watergate matter rest were on the staff of *The Washington Post*. Bob Woodward was a graduate of Yale and a Navy veteran, an

Ivy League type. By contrast, Carl Bernstein was a college drop-out who had worked his way up the journalistic ladder from copy boy to reporter. He seemed more at home with the counterculture of protest and rock concerts than his colleague. As investigative reporters, the two men, both in their late twenties, gathered pieces of information and tried to put them together, much the way people assemble parts of a jigsaw puzzle. Backed by their demanding executive editor, Ben Bradlee, and their tolerant publisher, Katherine Graham, they were determined to keep the Watergate story alive.[1] For Woodward and Bernstein, some nagging questions about the break-in remained. For starters, they wanted to know more about "E. Hunt W.H.," the name found in one of the burglar's notebooks. Who was he? Why was his name written in the notebook? What was his relationship to the burglars?

To find the answers to these and other questions, Bernstein and Woodward did research, checking into the background of the burglars and speaking to people they knew in government. Woodward got in touch with a confidential source high up in the Nixon administration. Reporters rarely disclose the names of their informants unless they are given permission to do so. Sometimes, people take great personal or professional risk when they tell reporters what they know or suspect. This is why Woodward and Bernstein agreed to keep their administration contact anonymous. He was given the alias Deep Throat, the title of a 1970s X-rated movie.[2] To this day, people wonder who Deep Throat was. The reporters have never revealed his name.

Woodward had to take elaborate precautions to avoid exposing Deep Throat's identity. To arrange meetings with him, Woodward relied on a variety of cloak-and-dagger techniques. For example, on some mornings Woodward placed a flower pot with a red flag planted in it on the balcony of his apartment. This was the prearranged signal that he wanted to see his informant. If Woodward did not hear anything during the day, he knew they would get together at two o'clock the following morning in an underground garage. Sometime after midnight Woodward would dash out of his apartment, sneak down a back alley, and take a cab for part of the distance. Anxiously, he would change to another taxi, looking over his shoulder to make sure no one was following him. Finally, he would arrive at the garage where Deep Throat waited. [3]

The two men could talk in privacy for a couple of hours. Over the course of their meetings, Deep Throat advised Woodward to look into the Watergate burglars' ties to the White House staff as well as to the CRP. He also suggested that the reporters trace the way the Watergate operation was financed. He urged them to check into the possibility of other illegal campaign activities. These conversations were immensely useful to The Washington Post reporters as they tried to put the pieces of the Watergate puzzle together.

With help from Deep Throat, Woodward and Bernstein discovered that E. Hunt was E. Howard Hunt, Jr., a White House consultant. Like McCord, Hunt was formerly a member of the CIA. Since the Watergate break-in, Hunt had mysteriously disappeared. The FBI had 150 operatives searching for him. He did not turn up until July 7. Gradually, the reporters came to realize that Hunt was not just an ordinary White House advisor, rather he was somehow involved in the president's reelection campaign. What he was actually doing was far removed from planning traditional fund-raising and vote-getting activities. He was deeply involved in intelligence-gathering missions. They found out that Hunt was trying to dig up embarrassing information about Senator Ted Kennedy's private life. The White House had been busily trying to block a possible Kennedy candidacy during the Democratic primaries. Intrigued, the reporters probed further. They also learned that Hunt had been investigating the background of Daniel Ellsberg. However, they did not find out that Hunt had been a member of the Plumbers unit until some months later.

Watergate burglars Frank Sturgis and Bernard Barker had interesting histories as well. Bernstein and Woodward discovered that these Miamians were among a group of men who tried to attack Daniel Ellsberg in May 1972, as he addressed a group of demonstrators. The group was protesting the Vietnam War on the steps of the Capitol. Several demonstrators were hurt, but the police stopped the attackers before the men could reach Ellsberg.[4] In view of what they had found out about Hunt's activities, the reporters thought it was more than a mere coincidence that two other figures from the Watergate break-in were also connected to Ellsberg.

The reporters soon discovered that Barker was linked to a CRP lawyer, G. Gordon Liddy. Before moving to CRP, Liddy, like Hunt, had worked on the White House staff. On July 25, the *New York Times* reported that, for three months prior to the break-in, Barker had made a number of phone calls from Miami to Liddy's office at CRP. Earlier *Newsday*, a local New York newspaper, had released a story that CRP director John Mitchell had fired Liddy for failing to answer FBI questions about the Watergate break-in. The administration had already decided to let Liddy take the blame for the break-in. They claimed that, while he was associated with CRP Liddy, in planning the burglary, had acted on his own, exceeding his authority.

There were other ties between Bernard Barker and the CRP. On July 31, the *New York Times* revealed that he had deposited and withdrawn huge sums of money from a bank account in Miami. This money was first traced to cashiers checks originating in Mexico City and ultimately to CRP's chief fund raiser and finance chairman, the former secretary of commerce Maurice Stans. Stans had been shipping funds to Mexico, where they were changed into anonymous cashiers checks and sent back to the United States. Stans was laundering unlawful campaign contributions, manipulating money to conceal its illegal source.

Using information from the *Times* story, the *Washington Post* reporters tried to trace the flow of funds at CRP. Piecing together information supplied by several sources, they found out that before Liddy had been fired, he had been placed in charge of a "convention security" fund at CRP which he could spend at his own discretion. Liddy had indeed received money from the slush fund in Maurice Stans's safe. (A slush fund consists of unaccounted money that is used for bribes and other politically corrupt purposes.) Could these facts explain another part of the Watergate puzzle the newsmen had been trying to piece together? They had learned that Howard Hunt's attorney received a prepaid fee of $25,000 in a plain brown envelope. Perhaps Hunt's attorney and burglar Bernard Barker had received money from the CRP "convention security" fund, which came from Stans's safe.

In mid-August, the curious reporters were able to uncover another interesting part of the Watergate puzzle. Informal interviews with some reluctant, low-level CRP staffers revealed a highly suspicious pattern of activities, suggesting a cover-up. What was it about Watergate that the administration was trying so desperately to hide? Reporters found out that shortly after the break-in attempt, many CRP records were destroyed. Moreover, FBI interviews of CRP personnel were always conducted at campaign headquarters in the presence of a lawyer for CRP. Staffers were instructed not to volunteer any information to the FBI. The federal agents asked superficial questions and neglected to follow them up. What the reporters did not find out was that L. Patrick Gray, acting director of the FBI, had even given John Dean daily reports of the investigation so that the president's men would know where they stood. Nevertheless, the information that reporters did gather was still quite damaging.

Then on August 22, the *Post* was able to report preliminary findings from the Government Accounting Office (GAO), Congress's official auditing agency. CRP had failed to report over $500,000 in campaign contributions, $100,000 of which was set aside in an illegal campaign security fund. The committee violated the new Federal Campaign Expenditures Act, which had gone into effect in April 1972. The law tightened limits on campaign contributions and required disclosure of all monies spent.

A week later, President Nixon felt the need to hold a press conference to defuse the explosive information that reporters and the GAO had turned up. The *Post* stories and GAO disclosures had put more pressure on the president and his men. With the election only two months away, they could not afford to have the Watergate matter blow up in their faces. On August 29, President Nixon held a question-and-answer session at his beachside estate in San Clemente, California. He expressed his faith in Maurice Stans and dismissed the GAO's findings by commenting, "With regard to the matter of handling campaign funds, we have a new law here in which technical violations have occurred and are occurring, apparently on both sides."[5]

To put the reporters' curiosity to rest and to reassure the public, he announced that an investigation of the Watergate break-in was in the hands of the FBI, the Department of Justice, a grand jury, and the General Accounting Office. He also mentioned that former attorney general John Mitchell had cleared CRP officials of any role in the burglary before he retired as director of the committee in July. He went on to say:

> *In addition to that, within our own staff, under my direction, the counsel to the President, Mr. Dean, has conducted a complete investigation of all leads which might involve any present members of the White House staff or anybody in the government. I can say categorically that his investigation indicates that no one in the White House staff, no one in this Administration, presently employed, was involved in this very bizarre incident.* [6]

However the president could not be taken at his word. Indeed, he had lied to the public. John Dean himself was surprised to learn that he had conducted a Watergate investigation. In fact, he had not. Overall, the president's remarks did little to discourage the reporters from pursuing the Watergate story.

On September 15, the grand jury indicted (formally charged) the five men arrested at Watergate and their masterminds, Hunt and Liddy, with burglary, conspiracy, and illegal wiretapping. During the grand jury investigation, witnesses had placed Hunt and Liddy at the Watergate complex during the time of the break-in. They also swore that Liddy had planned the burglary on his own. The president's men had decided to sacrifice Hunt and Liddy in order to protect themselves as well as the president's election campaign. The grand jury witnesses had been instructed to commit perjury.

A few days later, all seven Watergate defendants, the five burglars and Hunt and Liddy, pleaded innocent to the charges. In response to the indictments, Department of Justice officials issued the following statement: "We have absolutely no evidence to indicate that others should be charged."[7] In fact, Attorney General Kleindienst, as the head of the Justice Department, had done his best to limit the scope of the FBI's inquiry to protect members of the

CRP and the White House staff. Most of the reporters working on the case suspected that the indictment did not go far enough, but they had no inkling of the role Kleindienst had played, nor could they prove their suspicions.

On November 7, Americans went to the polls, giving little thought to the Watergate break-in or stories of illegal campaign activities carried in the press. They just shrugged their shoulders and ignored the charges and countercharges they read. Most Americans tend to be tolerant of irregularities at election time. They figure that somehow the best candidate has always won, despite all the fuss about frauds and dirty tricks. It was no surprise to them that on November 7, the president triumphed over his Democratic opponent, South Dakota senator George McGovern, winning 60.7 percent of the popular vote and gaining all the electoral votes except those of Massachusetts and the District of Columbia. The president was at the height of his popularity. He had recently returned from trips to China and Moscow. He had negotiated an arms reduction treaty with the Soviet Union. The unpopular Vietnam War appeared to be winding down. He looked like a certain winner long before Election Day.

For the next month or so after the election, reporters were unable to come up with any new stories on illegal funding or campaign intelligence activities. Then Carl Bernstein got lucky. He was able to interview a White House secretary who gave him an overview of the Nixon administration's intelligence-gathering activities. She had worked for the Plumbers unit. She stated for the record who the Plumbers were and what they had done. At last, the reporters could link Hunt and Liddy to the White House and to a series of illegal intelligence-gathering activities. On December 8, 1972, the *Washington Post* published Carl Bernstein's story on the White House Plumbers unit as part of an ongoing series about the Watergate break-in.

Shortly after the piece appeared, the newspaper was excluded from covering White House social events. Then the Federal Communications Commission (FCC), the broadcast licensing agency, received documents challenging the paper's ownership of two television stations. Around the same time the price of the *Post's* stock plummeted and lost almost half its value. Did this happen by coincidence or design? The newspaper's publisher, Katherine Graham, and executive editor, Ben Bradlee, were pretty certain that the *Post's* stories were coming close to the truth. They suspected that angry officials in the Nixon administration were orchestrating the attacks on the *Post* in retaliation for the damaging articles. They became even more determined to keep publishing whatever their reporters turned up, subject, of course, to verification.

On January 8, 1973, the Watergate trial opened. The presiding judge was sixty-eight-year-old John J. Sirica, nicknamed Maximum Sentence John because of the penalties he was known to impose. Once again, the press corps heard the administration's official story. Gordon Liddy had been given funds for legitimate intelligence-gathering activities. He had acted on his own when he arranged for the illegal bugging of the Democratic National Committee Headquarters. The only interesting development during the first week was that Howard Hunt changed his plea to guilty, and that came as no surprise to Carl Bernstein. Two days before the Watergate burglars were to stand trial, the reporter had visited one of the defendants. He learned that the men intended to plead not guilty and claim they had been working on a secret mission approved by high government officials. However, Bernstein was told that a plea of not guilty might have to be abandoned because Howard Hunt did not want to risk exposing other people in the break-in.

Over the weekend the *New York Times'* investigative reporter Seymour Hersh wrote an article revealing that CRP director John Mitchell had known about the break-in and had given it his support. Watergate defendant Frank Sturgis was Hersh's source for the story. Then *Time* magazine published a piece disclosing that the burglars had been promised payment for the time they had to spend in prison. This confirmed what Bernstein had already learned. He had found out that Hunt visited the burglars, urging the men he had recruited to admit to the crime in court. He promised them that their families would receive financial support while they were in jail and that they would be released after a few months. Was this why the men were willing to plead guilty and deny that higher-ups had advance knowledge of the break-in?

Since the arrest, the White House conspirators had been paying blackmail to Howard Hunt and the other burglars to keep them silent. Hunt had threatened to tell all he knew unless all seven defendants received a salary, additional money for their families, and lawyers' fees. A huge amount of money was involved which was beginning to drain the illegal funds Nixon's associates had collected. Then in early December, Hunt's wife died in an air crash. Ten thousand dollars of these secret sums was found in her purse. This time the money could not be traced to the White House or CRP. The Hunts had been paid with old used bills which had random serial numbers, and their paymaster had worn rubber gloves in handling them. Evidently, some lessons had been learned from the Watergate fiasco.

On Monday, the trial resumed. Predictably, the four burglars did change their plea to guilty. When government prosecutors limited themselves to a routine and superficial examination of the defendants, a skeptical Judge Sirica interrupted them and began to question the burglars himself. He queried them about the source of the $100 bills found during the break-in.

Barker replied, "I got the money in the mail in a blank envelope."

"Well, I'm sorry. I don't believe you," the judge retorted.

Asked whether they had ever worked for the CIA, Martinez responded, "Not that I know of." His answer was an outright lie.

When Judge Sirica demanded to know why the men had broken into the Watergate complex, Martinez answered, not too convincingly, "It pertained to the Cuban situation. When it comes to Cuba and when it comes to Communist conspiracies involving the United States, I will do anything to protect this country against any Communist conspiracy."

The judge wanted to know how the Democratic National Committee Headquarters was connected to a communist conspiracy. "I don't know," was all Martinez could say.

"Were you working under the direction of Mr. Hunt or other people in this job that was pulled off?" the judge asked, as he interrogated Barker.

"I was working with Mr. Hunt and I wish to state that I was completely identified with Mr. Hunt," came the reply.[8]

After Judge Sirica completed his interrogation, no wiser but more suspicious than he had been when he began, the five defendants were led off to jail.

Of the seven men indicted in the break-in, only McCord and Liddy still insisted that they were innocent of any crime. Their cases took up the remaining two weeks of the trial. As was expected, CRP officials glibly testified that Liddy had exceeded his authority and that no one else knew about plans for the break-in. One witness told Bob Woodward that he could have implicated Ehrlichman and John Dean in the burglary, but government prosecutors did not ask him the right questions. Instead, they treated the officials with great respect and did not subject them to a probing examination. The questions they asked were quite restricted in scope and produced uninformative answers.

After a sixteen-day trial, the jury, in just ninety minutes, found the defendants guilty of attempted burglary and eavesdropping. Sentencing was set for late March. Meanwhile an angry Judge Sirica criticized the prosecution for the way the case had been handled. He commented:

> *Everyone knows that there's going to be a congressional investigation in this case. I would frankly hope, not only as a judge but as a citizen of a great country and one of millions of Americans who are looking for certain answers, I would hope the Senate committee is granted the power by Congress by a broad enough resolution to try to get to the bottom of what happened in this case. . . .*[9]

For Judge Sirica and the Congress, the Watergate trial had ended, but the Watergate affair was far from over. In fact, it had only just begun. The grand jury that had indicted the burglars continued to investigate events surrounding the break-in.

Thanks to the untiring efforts of the press corps and their courageous informants, pieces of the Watergate puzzle were gradually falling into place. Reporters had exposed ties among the burglars, the CRP, and some low-level members of the White House staff. They had revealed the existence of illegal campaign finances to fund unlawful activities. However, the reporters suspected that the true story of the break-in was just beginning to unfold. They turned their attention to Congress and the Watergate grand jury who would sift rumors from facts. Despite the reporters' aggressive probes, members of the Nixon administration had succeeded in concealing much of what was going on from public scrutiny. Few knew that the president of the United States had played a major role in covering up the Watergate break-in.

STONEWALLING IT

The reporters had not been able to discover that within days of the bungled Watergate burglary, President Nixon had personally taken charge of the cover-up. In a series of memorable conversations, he revealed how he felt the break-in and cover-up should be handled. His first reaction was to protect his trusted advisors who were trapped in a messy situation. Not only did he approve of the way his aides had hidden their tracks, but also he suggested how they might improve their camouflage. By his actions, the president became an accomplice in an unlawful conspiracy to conceal a crime. Within days, he moved from knowledge of a concerted effort to cover up the break-in to active participation in the cover-up itself.

The president held many cover-up planning sessions in the Oval Office in the West Wing of the White House. It was a splendid room for a chief executive. Flagstands topped with gold eagles, their bright banners gathered in soft folds, stood as silent sentries. On the floor was a dark blue rug emblazoned with the gold presidential seal. Usually members of the White House staff would find Nixon seated in a large swivel chair with his feet resting on the huge mahogany presidential desk. He was utterly indifferent to the scars his heel marks left on the desk. He was comfortable, and that was all that mattered.

According to John Dean, a story about the president and his desk circulated around the White House. On one occasion, during Nixon's absence from the White House, the desk was sent out to be refinished. When the president returned and found the scars removed, he commented, "Dammit, I didn't order that! I want to leave *my* mark on this place just like other presidents."[1] His wish was granted.

It is clear that the president became involved in the Watergate cover-up almost from the start. Initially, his motive was to prevent anything from ruining his reelection campaign. On June 20, the president met with his legal counsel Charles Colson to discuss the Watergate situation. Boston attorney Colson had long been employed as a hatchetman, to conduct political warfare against the president's enemies. This is why he had recommended that Howard Hunt be transferred from the Plumbers unit to CRP. Richard Nixon set the tone for the cover-up when he told Colson, "I'm not going to worry about it. The hell with it. . . . At times, uh, I just stonewall it."[2] The term stonewall is an old British expression meaning to obstruct or to block. The president's men had already blocked efforts to expose their role in the Watergate affair by destroying evidence of the crime. The president endorsed their efforts. He was quite willing to obstruct justice, if necessary. (To obstruct justice means to prevent law enforcement officials from doing their job and to prevent the legal system from functioning as it should.) Throughout the entire Watergate affair, the president never abandoned this approach to the problem. He never considered the possibility of simply telling the truth. After all, the stakes were too great. At risk was his reelection. One lie soon fed upon another until the president and his men were in too deep to extricate themselves. By June 23, they were already in serious trouble.

That day, the president met with Chief of Staff Bob Haldeman for a follow up of an earlier conversation on June 20. Haldeman sat in the Oval Office, yellow pad in hand, ready to take notes. In this very important discussion, the president and his advisor covered a range of topics. According to the cover story that the president and his men had agreed upon earlier, the ringleader of the break-in, G. Gordon Liddy, would take the blame for the Watergate fiasco. If he could be made to seem an important figure, then, perhaps, investigators would not look any further into the question of who planned the failed break-in. In the following conversation with Haldeman, Nixon expressed some very interesting opinions about Liddy. The president also learned that CRP director John Mitchell was somehow involved in the break-in.

P   . . . Well, what the hell, did Mitchell know about this?

H   I think so. I don't think he knew the details, but I think he knew.

P   He didn't know how it was going to be handled though . . . Well who was the asshole that did? Is it Liddy? Is that the fellow? He must be a little nuts!

H   He is.

P   I mean he just isn't well screwed on, is he? Is that the problem?

H   No, but he was under pressure, apparently, to get more information, and as he got more pressure, he pushed people harder to move harder—

P   Pressure from Mitchell?

H   Apparently.[3]

Earlier in this same conversation, the two men considered what could happen if the investigation of the Watergate break-in proceeded much further. Then they devised a plot to take the FBI off the case. Haldeman told the president that Acting FBI Director L. Patrick Gray was having trouble controlling the bureau's veteran agents assigned to the break-in. Nixon learned that the FBI had already traced the money the burglars had in their possession. Through that money, the federal agents might link his close friend CRP director Mitchell to the break-in. Haldeman relayed Dean and Mitchell's suggestion that the CIA be called in to stop the FBI inquiry.

The president said, "[T]he way for us to handle this now is for us to have Walters call Pat Gray and just say, 'Stay to hell out of this—this is, ah, business here we don't want you to go any further on it.' That's not an unusual development, and ah, that would take care of it."[4] Walters was Vernon Walters, deputy director of the CIA, another old Nixon associate.

Not only did the president approve of the plan to call in the CIA, but also he came up with a scheme to make their intervention plausible. He devised a fictitious story Vernon Walters would be told to convince him to halt the FBI's probe. He instructed Haldeman: "[S]ay, 'Look the problem is that this will open the whole, the whole Bay of Pigs thing, and the President just feels that ah, without going into details—don't, don't lie to them to the extent to say there is no involvement, but just say this is a comedy of errors, without getting into it, . . ."[5]

At the Bay of Pigs, the CIA had led Cuban exiles into a doomed attempt to stir up a revolt against Fidel Castro's communist regime. Since former CIA operatives Hunt and the Cubans were under indictment as Watergate burglars, the president's idea was to suggest to the FBI that it should not interfere in a secret CIA-related activity by continuing to investigate the Watergate break-in. The fact that most of the story was a blatant lie did not trouble the president. He was just concerned about putting a stop to the investigation or, at least, containing it.

So, on June 23, in this one important conversation, President Nixon gave his approval to specific steps to obstruct justice, to prevent the FBI from doing its job. He even found a way to convince the CIA to call off the FBI. In effect, he made himself an accomplice in the conspiracy to cover up the Watergate break-in. For this offense he could be removed from office, although at the time, it did not appear that he realized the consequences of what he had done.

As soon as he had the president's approval, Haldeman put the plan in action. The very same day, at Haldeman's request, Vernon Walters asked Gray to suspend the investigation until the CIA was certain that no national security secrets would be revealed. However, once Walters satisfied himself that none of the Watergate burglars had been on the CIA's payroll for over two years, he refused to cooperate further with Haldeman. He refused to compromise the integrity of his organization.

As a result, the president had to rely on his staff and his appointees in the Department of Justice to keep the FBI from probing too deeply into the facts about Watergate. Although reporters were getting uncomfortably close to the truth about CRP and the break-in, Nixon was not discouraged. He simply announced to the press and the public that he knew nothing about the break-in and that no one in his administration had been involved in the crime. In his speeches and news conferences, he claimed that he was making every effort to get at the truth and bring the wrong-doers to justice.

By September 15, all these efforts seemed to be working. The Watergate grand jury had just handed down indictments. At this point, only the Watergate burglars and their ringleaders faced criminal charges for the break-in. The jury did not suspect that the president was orchestrating the cover-up. Privately, Richard Nixon was very pleased, so pleased that he and his chief of staff Bob Haldeman met with John Dean to congratulate him on his role in the cover-up.

P   Hi, how are you? You've had quite a day today didn't you. You got Watergate on the way, didn't you?

D   We tried.

H   How did it all end up?

D   Ah, I think we can say well at this point. The press is playing it just as we expected.

H   Whitewash?

D   No, not yet—the story right now—

P   It is a big story.

H   Five indicted plus the WH former guy and all that.

D   Plus two White House fellows.

H   That is good that takes the edge off whitewash really that was the thing Mitchell kept saying that to people in the country Liddy and Hunt were big men. Maybe that is good.[6]

Next, the three men took up the bugging of the Democratic National Headquarters. From their point of view, eavesdropping on political opponents was a normal and necessary activity. If Nixon had been consulted in advance, he would probably have given his consent to the plan to put electronic listening devices in the Democrats' Watergate offices.

P   Yes (expletive deleted), Goldwater [Republican Senator Barry Goldwater of Arizona] put it in perspective when he said (expletive deleted) everybody bugs everybody else. You know that.

D That was priceless.

P It happens to be totally true. We were bugged in '68 on the plane and in '62 even running for Governor—(expletive deleted) thing you ever saw.

D It is a shame that evidence to the fact that that happened in '68 was never around. I understand that only the former Director [J. Edgar Hoover, FBI director] had that information.

H No, that is not true.

D There was evidence of it?

H There are others who have information.

P How do you know? . . .[7]

Then the president went on to explain, "The difficulty with using it, of course, is it reflects on Johnson [President Lyndon B. Johnson]. If it weren't for that, I would use it. Is there any way we could use it without using his name—saying that the DNC [Democratic National Committee] did it? No—the FBI did the bugging."[8]

Nixon toyed with the idea of using the information that his plane was bugged during his 1968 presidential campaign to counteract the political benefits the Democrats were getting from the Watergate break-in. He wanted to show that the Democrats were not the innocent victims they claimed to be. In his private conversations, Nixon did not make moral judgments about eavesdropping on an opponent because, for him, it was not a moral question. What was moral to Nixon was winning the election and protecting his men. The American people did not seem to disagree with him.

The president and his aides went on to discuss how well they had managed to contain the Watergate affair.

With the trial coming up, they felt they had little to fear. Dean even boasted that the cover-up was so successful that the embarrassing problem of the break-in would soon disappear.

D   Three months ago, I would have had trouble predicting there would be a day when this would be forgotten, but I think I can say that 54 days from now [when the trial would be held] nothing is going to come crashing down to our surprise.

P   That what?

D   Nothing is going to come crashing down to our surprise.

P   Oh well, this is a can of worms, as you know a lot of this stuff that went on. And the people who worked this way are awfully embarrassed. But the way you have handled all this seems to me has been skillful putting your finger in the leaks that have sprung here and sprung there.[9]

Indirectly, the president was praising Dean for coaching witnesses appearing before the grand jury, as well as the people the FBI was questioning. He also valued Dean's role as a troubleshooter. Dean had access to FBI reports of the investigation, so he could second-guess what the FBI would do next and take measures to see that the investigation did not get out of control. Dean had obstructed justice. For this the president praised him. Other chief executives might have condemned him, but then other chief executives might not value stonewalling as highly as President Nixon did.

Then the president and his men turned their attention to the friction the Watergate situation had created within their own ranks and between themselves and their Democratic opponents. Theirs was a very revealing dialogue.

D   On this case. There is some bitterness between the Finance Committee and the Political Committee—they feel they are taking all the heat and all the people upstairs are bad people—not being recognized.

P   We are all in it together. This is a war. We take a few shots and it will be over. We will give them a few shots and it will be over. Don't worry, I wouldn't want to be on the other side right now. Would you?

D   Along that line, one of the things I've tried to do, I have begun to keep notes on a lot of people, who are emerging as less than our friends because this will be over some day and we shouldn't forget that way some of them have treated us.

P   I want the most comprehensive notes on all those who tried to do us in. They didn't have to do it. If we had a very close election and they were playing the other side, I would understand this. No—they were doing this quite deliberately and they are asking for it, and they are going to get it. We have not used the power in this first four years as you know. We have never used it. We have not used the Bureau and we have not used the Justice Department but things are going to change now. And they are either going to do it right or go.[10]

The president was willing to abuse the powers of his office, to violate his inaugural oath, by using the FBI and the Department of Justice to get even with the people who let him down. As he admitted, politics was a war, and in a war, Richard Nixon believed that any means was permissible. Of course, the Constitution had been written for the very purpose of defining which means were acceptable and which were not, but the vengeful president did not concern himself with constitutional limits.

As their conversation drew to a close, Dean assured the president that in any case the Justice Department did not plan to use the GAO's findings on campaign fund irregularities against the administration or its opponents. He also mentioned that he had put a stop to Senator Ted Kennedy's plan to have his Administrative Practices subcommittee look into that problem.

P   You really can't sit and worry about it all the time. The worst may happen but it may not. So you just try to button it up as well as you can and hope for the best, and remember basically the damn business is unfortunately trying to cut our losses.

D   Certainly that is right and certainly it has had no effect on you. That's the good thing.

H   No, it has been kept away from the White House and of course completely from the President. . . .[11]

However, Dean warned that a new threat to the cover-up was looming. Democrat Wright Patman of Texas, chairman of the House Banking and Currency Committee, wanted to investigate the Watergate affair. The president approved Dean and Haldeman's suggestion that Watergate defendants' lawyers should complain that the publicity that the hearings would receive would deny their clients a fair trial. Dean mentioned that they were also approaching a member of the American Civil Liberties Union (ACLU), a liberal organization dedicated to fair play, to support the complaint. Ironically, the administration was doing its best to make sure the Watergate burglars would not get a fair trial. Members of the White House staff had concealed or destroyed evidence and were doing their best to limit the scope of the criminal investigation.

The president also accepted another idea his advisors proposed. They would try to get Republicans in the House of Representatives to convince members of Patman's committee to call off the hearings. In response to intense political pressure, on October 3, committee members voted 20–15 against their chairman's plans to investigate the break-in. Nixon and his staff were relieved that they would not face a congressional inquiry before the November elections.

The president swept the 1972 elections. Despite media exposés linking the president's men to the break-in, the American people had shown at the polls that they were willing to ignore a campaign prank like Watergate. They had reelected Richard Nixon by an overwhelming margin of victory. Then the trial of the Watergate defendants was brought to a successful conclusion. However, these events brought little relief to the president's men. New worries soon replaced old ones.

Now, the Democratic leadership in the Senate was determined to find out what the Watergate trial had concealed. Since Wright Patman's vain attempt to inquire into the matter ended in October, congressional suspicions of wrongdoing had been steadily mounting. On February 7, by a unanimous vote of 77–0, the Senate set up a committee to investigate the Watergate affair and 1972 campaign finances. They voted it $500,000 for expenses. Constitutional scholar Senator Sam Ervin of South Carolina agreed to serve as chairman. The committee would hold closed sessions until May 17. Then they intended to hold public hearings.

The president's men realized that they would be in great trouble if the senators ever started to question what had happened after the break-in took place. Discovery of the Watergate cover-up they had engineered might also lead to the exposure of their other illegal activities. They needed a new approach to the cover-up. The public could ignore what had happened at the Democratic National Committee Headquarters. What it would find more difficult to forgive or forget was that a president of the United States had persistently lied to them and had actually directed the Watergate cover-up. For them, the true crime would prove to be not the break-in but the cover-up.

4

A CAP ON
THE BOTTLE

During the spring of 1973, threats to expose the Watergate cover-up were mounting from many different sides. Richard Nixon and his advisors had to fend off preliminary staff demands for information from the Senate's Watergate Committee, damaging leaks from the ongoing grand jury investigation, and aggressive probing by the press corps. Within the administration, tensions were rising as the White House aides sought to protect themselves and the president from exposure. The risks of disclosure increased with every passing day. So did the feverish planning sessions to counteract them.

The president's men were already under pressure. They had to fund continued blackmail payments to the Watergate burglars. Then there were unwelcome surprises, such as embarrassing revelations at hearings before the Senate Judiciary Committee, an unexpected letter to Judge Sirica, and defections among the president's men. A web of circumstantial evidence gradually tightened around the White House staff until it threatened the president himself. What was striking was that in the midst of the turmoil, the president rarely questioned whether a proposed course of action was right, whether it was legal. Rather, he worried about how it would look, how well it would serve as a public relations gesture.

On February 28, the president and John Dean began a series of strategy sessions to deal with the immediate problems they faced. It was the first time they had met since September 15. Bob Haldeman and John Ehrlichman sat in on some of their conversations. The men realized that Judge Sirica would be sentencing the Watergate burglars in a few weeks. The judge had offered reduced sentences to any defendant who would tell him what was really going on. It was important that the burglars remain silent. Sam Ervin's Senate committee would be waiting to pounce on any information they might offer the judge.

D   There is every indication that they are hanging in tough right now.

P   What the hell do they expect though? Do they expect clemency in a reasonable time? What would you advise on that?

D   I think it is one of those things we will have to watch very closely. For example, —

P   You couldn't do it, say, in six months?

D   No you couldn't. This thing may become so political as a result of these hearings that it is a vendetta. The judge may go off the deep end in sentencing . . .[1]

The president had the constitutional right to pardon criminals. This is why he debated the idea of clemency with Dean. As a promise to the burglars, it could usefully buy their continued silence, but it would further involve him in efforts to obstruct justice. The president was not worried about the legal problem, but he did hesitate. What he feared was how his decision might affect his public image. How might the public react if he pardoned the men before the congressional elections of 1974? As he weighed the pros and cons, he reached no firm decision.

The discussion then turned to the Senate hearings. The men were trying to figure out what position to take. Should they take the offensive or the defensive when asked to comment on the proceedings? The president indicated that his approach was "to say nothing about the hearings at this point, except that I trust they will be conducted the proper way and I will not comment on the hearings while they are in progress. . . . We'll see as time goes on. Maybe we will have to change our policy. But the President should not become involved in any part of the case."[2] The president did not want to have to answer every charge that witnesses before the Senate might make. If he responded, the charges would receive even more damaging publicity.

On March 13, the president, Dean, and Haldeman were working on a way to handle the Ervin committee hearings. Should they appear to cooperate with the Senate staff or man their battle stations and resist the investigators' demands for information? The president defined his position to his two aides: "We said we will furnish information, but we are not going to be called to testify. That is the position. Dean and all the rest will grant you information. Won't you?"[3]

To keep his aides from appearing as witnesses before the Watergate Committee, the president was relying on executive privilege. (Executive privilege is the claim that it is in the national interest to keep secret from the public or other branches of government private presidential conversations and documents.) The president would permit members of the White House staff to cooperate by submitting written information to the senators. This was one effective way to limit the scope of the committee's investigation and to avoid having to answer probing questions. Richard Nixon would project an image of a helpful chief executive concerned with the constitutional doctrine of separation of powers. According to this doctrine, each branch of government—the executive, the legislative, and the judicial—had the right to protect its operations from unjustified meddling by the other branches. The Constitution did not mean by this that each branch of government could ignore the others and do what it pleased. Each had to cooperate with the other, and each was entitled to interfere with the others in certain areas. This is why the Constitution also included the doctrine of "checks and balances." In this instance, the president was not really concerned with the constitutional issues; he was more concerned with protecting his men.

The president also extended executive privilege to cover White House staff appearances before the Senate Judiciary Committee. This committee was holding hearings on whether L. Patrick Gray should be confirmed as permanent director of the FBI. During his testimony on March 7, L. Patrick Gray had revealed an explosive piece of information. In an effort to appear totally honest and sincere before the examining senators, Gray accidentally let it slip that he had given John Dean FBI reports during the FBI's Watergate investigation. Now Nixon decided that it was necessary to prevent further senate inquiries into Gray's troublesome admission by invoking executive privilege. The president explained, "That is what I would say: that is, what I would prepare in the press thing. He [Dean] will respond under oath in a letter. He will not appear in a formal session."4 As a result, Gray's testimony would be neither confirmed nor denied. By April, the acting director's nomination was withdrawn, and William Ruckelshaus took over until Clarence B. Kelley was approved for the post.

On March 21, Nixon, Dean, and Haldeman held another lengthy and crucial discussion, one of the most important talks they ever had. Their conversation ranged over a number of "loaded" topics, including continued payments to silence Hunt and the Watergate burglars, perjury committed by Nixon's aides, and the need for a new strategy to hide the cover-up. As they spoke, the president seemed to behave more and more like a conspirator in an illegal enterprise. This was ironic since during his campaign for reelection he had pledged to be the nation's chief defender of law and order. Richard Nixon was still in a position to tell the prosecutors all that he knew and come out of the situation relatively unblemished. However, from the president's point of view, he would be surrendering to his political opponents and displaying disloyalty to the men who had served him so faithfully. He was not prepared to do this—yet.

D   I think there is no doubt about the seriousness of the problem we've got. We have a cancer within, close to the Presidency, that is growing. . . . Basically, it is because (1) we are being blackmailed; (2) People are going to start perjuring themselves very quickly that have not had to perjure themselves to protect other people in the line. And there is no assurance—

P   That it won't bust?[5]

Dean outlined the way the Watergate plan took shape and gave the president the names of all the people who had turned Liddy loose at the elegant Watergate complex. This may have been the first time the president was supplied with all the details. Nixon also learned that Mitchell and Magruder lied to the Watergate grand jury. Dean went on to explain that payments had been made to silence the burglars and that these blackmail demands were continuing. He made it clear that both perjury and blackmail were obstructions of justice, but the president did not seem worried about that.

P   How much money do you need?
D   I would say these people are going to cost a million dollars over the next two years.
P   We could get that. On the money, if you need the money you could get that. You could get a million dollars. You could get it in cash. I know where it could be gotten. . . .[6]

The president did not object to paying the blackmail money. In all, the subject of blackmail came up about ten times during the conversation, and each time the president expressed no qualms about the payments or the mounting expense. He assured his aides that they could easily get hold of the money when it was needed. What he did object to was the possibility that the Watergate burglars might tell what they knew.

P   Just looking at the immediate problem, don't you think you have to handle Hunt's financial situation damn soon?
D   I think that is—I talked with Mitchell about that last night and—
P   It seems to me we have to keep the cap on the bottle that much, or we don't have any options.[7]

Dean seemed less optimistic about the success of the Watergate cover-up than he had been in his previous talks with the president.

D   I am not confident that we can ride through this. I think there are soft spots.

P   You used to be—
D   I am not comfortable for this reason. I have noticed of recent—since the publicity has increased on this thing again, with the Gray hearings, that everybody is now starting to watch after their behind. . . .
P   They are scared.[8]

The president came to realize that even if his men stood firm, their secretaries and assistants might eventually tell all they knew. There was little he could do about that. However, in view of the threats of disclosure the president and his men faced from the Ervin committee and the possible confession of one of the Watergate burglars in exchange for a lighter sentence, it became obvious to him that a new cover-up strategy was needed.

To present the facts from the administration's point of view, the president came up with the idea of the so-called Dean Report. Back in August, the president had credited Dean with the nonexistent report. Now, during this prolonged discussion, Nixon told Dean, Ehrlichman, and Haldeman that he actually wanted a written account of the Watergate burglary. Committed to stonewalling the Watergate affair, the president thought that he could solve the problem of potential Watergate Committee revelations with a public relations strategy. He would use the Dean Report to tell part of the truth while hiding the whole picture.

> *I asked for a written report, which I do not have, which is very general understand, I am thinking now in far more general terms, having in mind the facts, that where specifics are concerned make it very general, your investigation of the case. Not that "this man is guilty, this man is not guilty," but "this man did do that."* [9]

The president went on to find other benefits of the Dean Report. It could be used to disarm L. Patrick Gray's admission that Dean had received FBI reports during the Watergate investigation.

> *This also helps with the Gray situation because it shows Dean's name on the FBI reports as reporting to the President. He can say in there, "I have not disclosed the contents of these to anybody else."*[10]

The report could also be given to the Ervin committee as a symbol of the administration's efforts to cooperate with the Congress while protecting itself from unwanted questions by executive privilege.

No matter how hard he tried, over the next few weeks, Dean was unable to draft the report for the president. It was difficult to pin the blame for the crime on any one of the president's men without implicating the others. There was no way to reveal some of the Watergate story without raising questions about what had been left out.

While Dean was working on the report, the president and his men continued their meetings. A major new problem had arisen. On March 23, Judge Sirica released the text of a letter he had received from convicted Watergate burglar John McCord, due for sentencing the next day. Sirica had offered more lenient sentences to any of the men who offered to reveal what had actually led to the Watergate break-in. McCord had written:

> *Several members of my family have expressed fear for my life if I disclose knowledge of the facts in this matter either publicly or to any Government representative.*
>
> *Whereas I do not share their concerns to the same degree, nevertheless, I do believe that retaliatory measures will be taken against me, my family, and my friends should I disclose such facts.*[11]

He went on to admit that the defendants had been pressured to plead guilty, and that during the trial, witnesses had committed perjury. After publication of the letter, McCord was asked to appear before the Ervin committee. The president phoned John Dean and conceded there was no way to keep a "cap on the bottle."[12]

On March 27, in a conversation with Ehrlichman and Haldeman, the reluctant president realized that he would have to sacrifice his close friend John Mitchell along with Jeb Magruder, deputy director of CRP. The president and Mitchell worked together in a New York law firm for five years after Nixon's defeat for the California governorship. Mitchell had gone on to direct Nixon's successful presidential bids as well as to serve him as attorney general. Nevertheless, Nixon would let Mitchell and Magruder take responsibility for the break-in. Reporters, having gotten wind of McCord's revelations to Ervin committee investigators, were already linking the two men to the Watergate scandal.

P   Well, what is Mitchell's option, though? You mean to say—let's see what he could do. Does Mitchell come in and say, "My memory is faulty. I lied?"

E   No. He can't say that. He says,—ah, ah—

P   "That without intending to, I may have been responsible for this, and I regret it very much but I did not realize what they were up to. They were—we were—talking about apples and oranges." That's what I think he would say. Don't you agree?

H   I think so. He authorized apples and they bought oranges. Yeah.

P   Mitchell, you see, is never never going to go in and admit perjury. I mean, he may say he forgot about Hunt, Liddy and all the rest, but he is never going to do that.

H   They won't give him that convenience, I wouldn't think, unless they figure they are going to get you. He is as high up as they've got.

E   He's the big Enchilada.

H   And he's the one the magazines zeroed in on this weekend.

P   They did? What grounds?

H   Yeah. (unintelligible) has a quote that they maybe have a big fish on the hook.

P   I think Mitchell should come down. [13]

Ever loyal, John Mitchell stoically plotted how he could testify before the Watergate grand jury and still protect the president. A frightened Jeb Magruder, however, having seen the handwriting on the wall, ran to the investigating authorities to confess his role in the scandal.

Fearing a plot by Haldeman and Ehrlichman to make him take the blame for Watergate in their place and worrying that Magruder might name him as the brains behind the cover-up, John Dean decided to save his own neck. On April 8, he phoned Haldeman and said that he was considering confessing what he knew. He did not inform Haldeman that he had already started to tell all he knew to the investigators. Haldeman warned him, "Once the toothpaste is out of the tube, it's going to be very hard to get it back in." [14]

Once Dean and Magruder defected, the president and his remaining aides knew they faced serious trouble. Not only would the facts of the Watergate break-in be exposed, but the existence of the cover-up would become public knowledge. The cover-up would dominate the Ervin hearings and Watergate grand jury investigations. By comparison, the break-in would become just a trivial event. The president and his men needed to make a decision about cover-up strategy quickly. Just how much of it could they reveal to the public? Who should be made the scapegoat for the growing scandal? How could they prevent exposure of some of their other illegal activities? The president knew that the White House had to get out its own version of events before the public got wind of what was really going on. Somehow, the press corps dug up what witnesses said behind the closed doors of the grand jury room or at closed sessions with the Watergate Committee staff. Since cover-up was at risk, the whole focus of the president's strategy had to shift. However, all he could come up with was a revised version of the so-called Dean Report. This time, Ehrlichman was assigned to do the writing.

In another series of conversations throughout the month of April, the conspirators plotted to discredit Dean's testimony before the grand jury. They also wanted to defuse the damage he and Magruder could do when the public Watergate hearings began. Dean knew far too much and could direct the cover-up investigation to the president himself. For example, Dean could link the president to the blackmail pay-offs to the Watergate defendants in order to buy time.

As he wrestled with the problem, the president suggested that they develop a cover story that the payments were made for compassionate reasons: to help defendants with their lawyers' fees and to support their families.[15] Then he wavered and said the payments had to be concealed. He was groping for a way to justify his authorization of the payments, to justify his role in the entire cover-up. His efforts were confused and unsuccessful, and events soon overtook him.

As a result of Magruder and Dean's confessions, on April 15, Attorney General Kleindienst informed the president that Ehrlichman and Haldeman could be indicted for their roles in the Watergate affair. When Nixon discussed the problem with the two aides, they offered to resign, but the president was not yet willing to part with them. On April 17, a desperate President Nixon decided to make a public statement in an effort to protect them. His hands trembled as he read his prepared text. He announced that he was withdrawing his claim to executive privilege. In doing so, Nixon submitted to the inevitable since some of his aides were already giving information to members of the Ervin committee staff. Then he went on to state:

> On March 21st, as a result of serious charges which came to my attention, some of which were publicly reported, I began intensive new inquiries into this whole matter. . . .
>
> I can report today that there have been major developments in the case concerning which it would be improper to be more specific now, except to say that real progress has been made in finding the truth.
>
> If any person in the Executive Branch or in the government is indicted by the Grand Jury, my policy will be to immediately suspend him. If he is convicted, he will, of course, be automatically discharged. . . .
>
> As I have said before and I have said throughout this entire matter, all government employees and especially White House staff employees are expected fully to cooperate in this matter. I condemn any efforts to cover up in this case, no matter who is involved. [16]

In his statement, the president was claiming that he had known nothing about the Watergate cover-up until March 21. However, his private conversations with his advisors on June 20, June 23, September 15, February 28, etc., clearly contradict him. Once more, in the guise of telling the public the truth, he was, at best, telling another partial truth. The announcement he had made bought time, but it solved few of the president's problems. He still had reason to fear that Dean would tell investigators the full content of their conversations on the cover-up. He had to protect Haldeman and Ehrlichman as well as himself from the damage Dean could do.

On April 27, he tried to enlist the help of Assistant Attorney General Henry Petersen to stop Dean from talking. He wanted Petersen to deny Dean's request for immunity from prosecution in exchange for testimony. (Immunity, full or partial, protects informants from the full penalties the law can exact.) Some of the men suspected of wrongdoing in Watergate were already seeking out the prosecutor, trying to trade their testimony for reduced sentences. The president did not want Dean to receive immunity.

HP   Yes. Let me make myself clear.
P   Yes.
HP   I regard immunity authority under the statutes of the United States to be my responsibility, of which I cannot divest myself.
P   Right.
HP   And—ah—we take opinions, but I would have to treat this as advisory only. [17]

In effect, Petersen had stood up to the president and told him that he was under the command of the law, not the president. He could not guarantee that he would deny Dean immunity. Within a few days of this conversation, a very unhappy Richard Nixon finally concluded that since he could not prevent Dean from talking, he would have to sacrifice Haldeman and Ehrlichman in order to protect himself. Dean knew too much. This time, the president asked for and received letters of resignation from his two loyal aides.

A presidential advisor, attorney Leonard Garment, had been urging Nixon to fire them. Garment, along with John Mitchell, was one of Nixon's former New York law partners. Garment also recommended that the president appoint Elliot Richardson to replace Attorney General Richard Kleindienst, who had also been compromised by his role in the Watergate cover-up. Earlier in his career at the Justice Department, Kleindienst had antagonized the president because he had refused to replace members of his department with Nixon loyalists.

On April 30, the president made a series of admissions on nationwide television. Again, he was only telling partial truths. To separate himself from the Watergate scandal, he reminded his audience that he had been in Florida at the time of the break-in. He claimed that at first he had not believed the charges that some members of his administration and officials at CRP had participated in the Watergate affair. He dismissed the lies he had been telling the public all along by explaining that his previous comments about Watergate had been based on his staff's denials of guilt—which he had believed. In March, he went on,

> [N]ew information then came to me which persuaded me that there was a real possibility that some of these charges were true, and suggesting further that there had been an effort to conceal the facts both from the public, from you, and from me.
>
> As a result, on March 21, I personally assumed the responsibility for coordinating intensive new inquiries into the matter, and I personally ordered those

conducting the investigations to get all the facts and to report them directly to me, right here in this office. [18]

Once again, the president claimed to have known nothing of the cover-up until March 21. He was admitting to the public only what they already knew from newspaper accounts of the grand jury and preliminary Watergate investigations.

The president said he had accepted the resignations of Haldeman and Ehrlichman, "two of the finest public servants it has been my privilege to know." [19] He stated that he regretted the departure of Kleindienst, but mentioned the resignation of John Dean without further comment. Actually, Dean had been fired. Long after they left the White House, Haldeman and Ehrlichman did their best to discredit Dean's testimony. He could hurt them and reveal the president's role in the whole affair. However, they did not succeed.

The president announced the appointment of Elliot Richardson to be attorney general. Richardson had previously served Nixon as secretary of health, education, and welfare and as secretary of defense. Alexander Haig, a career army officer who had been a foreign affairs aide to Nixon's national security advisor, was named chief of staff. At Haig's suggestion, Nixon named Frederick Buzhardt, a Pentagon attorney, to serve as his counsel for Watergate matters. These able men would carry out the president's policies, but they were not devoted to Richard Nixon personally, the way Haldeman and Ehrlichman had been.

The president chose not to share with these men the full extent of his participation in the Watergate cover-up. He could not depend on them to protect him personally from the risks of exposure the Watergate hearings presented. Thus he made it very difficult for them to defend him. As he carried out his presidential duties, Richard Nixon soon had cause to worry that the senators would discover just how deeply he was involved in the cover-up. There was concrete evidence that he knew about the cover-up, evidence he thought they never would find.

5

THE SATURDAY NIGHT
MASSACRE

During the spring and summer of 1973, the Watergate scandal became a three-ring circus with a "cast of thousands." It was gradually transformed from a secret attempt to eavesdrop on the Democratic National Committee Headquarters into a huge public spectacle. In the first ring were the media. Their constant coverage of the Washington scene brought the public daily revelations of wrongdoing. The Senate's Watergate Committee occupied the second ring. Witness after witness began parading into the Senate caucus room to offer his version of events, each disclosing yet another shocking aspect of the Watergate cover-up. In the third ring was the legal system. Prosecutors and grand jurors busily gathered evidence against participants in the Watergate cover-up, members of the Plumbers unit, and political operatives who carried out other dubious projects in the hope of reelecting their president by a wide margin of victory. Those charged with the crimes came to trial. The courts also ruled on conflicts over evidence that Congress and a government prosecutor demanded from an unyielding administration.

As ringmaster, the defensive Richard Nixon tried to orchestrate events. The president fiercely protected his right to keep private his confidential conversations with White House advisors. He was willing to take desperate measures to fend off those he perceived as his antagonists. He underestimated the tenacity of his opponents. He also misjudged the reaction of public opinion to the steps he took.

The immediate focus of public attention was Democrat Sam Ervin of North Carolina. A folksy man, with a large face and bushy eyebrows, he looked as if he would be "far more comfortable in a rocking chair"[1] than in the chairman's seat, banging the gavel at committee meetings. However, this Harvard-trained lawyer had an impressive knowledge of the Constitution. In his middle seventies, Ervin was about to preside over the Senate Select Committee on Presidential Campaign Activities, otherwise known as the Watergate Committee. Congress sets up select committees on a temporary basis for special purposes.

This select committee contained four Democrats and three Republicans. Besides Ervin, the Senate Democrats included Daniel Inouye of Hawaii, Joseph Montoya of New Mexico, and Herman Talmadge of Georgia. The Republicans were committee vice chairman Howard Baker of Tennessee, Edward Gurney of Florida, and Lowell Weicker of Connecticut. Samuel Dash, an expert on wire tapping, served as the committee's chief counsel and staff director. At the peak of the investigation, the staff outnumbered the senators by almost fourteen to one.

From February to May, the senators and the committee staff had held executive, or closed, sessions in the auditorium of the Senate Office Building. They set to work interviewing witnesses and preparing for public hearings. They had three months to marshal their facts and trace the many threads of the conspiracy before the public hearings were scheduled to begin. Without their new computer, they would have had a hard time keeping track of all the names, places, and events that the witnesses recalled. While they were at work, on April 27, a California judge belatedly received a long-postponed Department of Justice memo describing White House staff members' role in the break-in at the office of Ellsberg's psychiatrist. He promptly dismissed all charges against Daniel Ellsberg for releasing *The Pentagon Papers* on grounds of government misconduct. About a year later a federal grand jury indicted members of the Plumbers unit for their role in that break-in.

On May 17, a few weeks after the charges against Ellsberg were dropped, the Ervin committee held its first public hearing in the huge, columned caucus room of the Old Senate Office Building. Overhead the ornate crystal chandeliers sparkled, but their brilliance was eclipsed by the rows of spotlights television crews had put up. These added heat as well as light. The seven senators were seated at one end of the overcrowded room. Before them were tables for witnesses and their lawyers as well as spectators. Television cameramen stood to the rear of the throng. A basic decision was made to start from the bottom up and build the case from there. Among the first witnesses to appear were the CRP office manager and one of the policemen who arrested the Watergate intruders. During the same week, burglars McCord and Barker also offered sworn statements about their roles in the Watergate affair.

At the same time that the senators were listening to this early testimony, the press was stealing their thunder. Newspapers and television carried stories about what the committee examiners had already uncovered in executive session. The effect of these articles and newscasts was so damaging to the White House that on May 22 President

Nixon released a 4,000-word statement professing his innocence. However, in keeping with his tactic of telling partial truths, he admitted that he had ordered restrictions placed on the burglary investigation in the interests of national security.

> It did seem to me to be possible that, because of the involvement of former CIA personnel, and because of some of their apparent associations, the investigation could lead to the uncovering of covert CIA operations totally unrelated to the Watergate break-in. [2]

Then he claimed, "It was certainly not my intent, nor my wish, that the investigation of the Watergate break-in or of related acts be impeded in any way."[3] The president's efforts to manipulate public opinion did little to restore confidence in his administration.

When it was CRP deputy director Jeb Magruder's turn to talk to the Senate committee members, attention returned to the public hearings. Magruder shocked most people when he confessed that former attorney general John Mitchell had given him the authority to place eavesdropping equipment in the Democratic National Committee Headquarters. However, Magruder's confession was only the prelude to more dramatic testimony. In late June, John Dean spoke before the assembled committee. It was then that Richard Nixon's worst fears were realized. Speaking of his September 15 conversation with the president, Dean stated, "I left with the impression that the President was well aware of what had been going on regarding the success of keeping the White House out of the Watergate scandal, and I also had expressed to him my concern that I was not confident the cover-up could be maintained indefinitely."[4]

Later, when the faithful Haldeman and Ehrlichman

gave their version of events, they could do little to discredit Dean's sensational revelations. The senators went on to other lesser figures in the scandal. As the questioning proceeded, vice chairman of the committee Howard Baker of Tennessee was heard repeatedly asking, "What did the president know, and when did he know it?" His question became a popular tag line for comedians as well as serious news commentators. Soon everyone was echoing his query.

The question was no longer a rhetorical one after Alexander Butterfield testified before the committee on July 16. This tall, weary Haldeman aide changed the whole course of the Watergate proceedings. He had confided some astounding information to the committee staff, which they had managed to keep secret from prying reporters. Based on this prior knowledge, at the public session he was asked, "Mr. Butterfield, are you aware of the installation of any listening devices in the Oval Office of the President?"

"I was aware of listening devices, yes, sir," came the reply. [5]

In the caucus room, the electrified spectators sat on the edge of their seats. Silently, they absorbed the news that the president's conversations in the White House and the Executive Office Building had been recorded on tape. In February 1971, Nixon had had the taping system installed, but he was not the first president to have had his conversations secretly recorded. He was following the example of Franklin D. Roosevelt, John F. Kennedy, and Lyndon B. Johnson. However, Nixon deployed his sophisticated taping equipment more extensively and used it more frequently than his predecessors had.

To date, the Ervin committee had collected only sworn statements about the president's role in the Watergate cover-up. Tapes of Nixon's discussions with his aides could provide them with direct evidence of the president's innocence or guilt. On July 17, Ervin wrote to the president requesting the tapes, but on the twenty-third, he was turned down. Then the chairman issued subpoenas (legal orders) to compel the president to give the committee five taped conversations and other documents. The White House chose to contest the committee's subpoenas in court. It had taken less than half an hour for Butterfield to tell the committee about the Dictabelt machines that recorded the president's conversations, but it would take many months for congressional investigators to find out exactly what the president knew and when he knew it.

Back in June, while Dean was still testifying, the president had started to listen to the tapes in the hope of finding evidence to disprove his former aide's accusations. At first, he thought he had statements to show that Dean was lying under oath to the Watergate committee. However, when lawyers heard his summaries, they explained that what the president found could easily be turned against him. Statements authorizing payment of blackmail funds to Howard Hunt could only damage the president's position. They would not make him appear as a compassionate man concerned for the families of the Watergate burglars.

On July 18, Richard Nixon had the taping system disconnected. Only gradually did the president realize that he would be in serious trouble if the recorded materials ever fell into the wrong hands. He decided that he would never hand over the tapes. The cost of sticking to this decision would be very high. If Nixon refused to turn over the tapes, he might be ousted from the presidency. However, if he did release them, he would certainly have to leave office.

Why Richard Nixon did not get rid of the tapes before the Watergate hearings started, no one knows and may never know. If he had, he might have saved his presidency. Perhaps he wanted to preserve for history an oral record of his administration. Perhaps, he had forgotten the many compromising conversations the tapes contained. Once the Ervin committee met, however, the president could not destroy them. Then, he would have been guilty of destroying evidence. Even Richard Nixon was not willing to go that far. As a matter of fact, when Rabbi Baruch Korff visited the president in mid-December and bluntly asked him why he had not disposed of the tapes, the president looked surprised at the question. Then he laughed the question aside and joked, "Where were you eight months ago?"[6]

As the Watergate story unfolded in the skilled hands of the senators and their staff, the public heard about Nixon's enemies list, a roster of about three hundred people, compiled by administration loyalists. They took down the names of contributors to Democratic causes and unfriendly journalists. CBS correspondent Daniel Schorr was number 17 on the list. In a 1971 broadcast, he had cast doubt on President Nixon's promised aid to parochial schools by commenting, "We can only assume the president's statement was for political or rhetorical effect."[7] The president was understandably angry; however, what happened next is best characterized as an overreaction to a passing provocation. Haldeman told his own assistant about the president's outburst. The assistant immediately phoned the FBI and insisted that a background check be done on the offending correspondent. The next day, within a seven-hour period, one FBI agent visited Schorr's office, another contacted the president of CBS, and yet others interviewed twenty-five of Schorr's friends, family, and co-workers. Was this a national security investigation, as the administration claimed, or harassment?

The public got quite an education in underhanded

espionage techniques, as perfected by members of the Plumbers unit and other political operatives. These men made the instruments of government serve purposes that the Constitution never intended. Wiretaps had been placed on Morton Halperin, an aide to National Security Advisor Henry Kissinger, and on State Department personnel in the hope of tracing and plugging leaks to the press. In the past, the government had restricted its eavesdropping to foreign diplomats and members of organized crime syndicates.

The Senate hearings showed how far political campaigning had come from kissing babies and shaking hands. The public found out that executives of large corporations were forced to make secret contributions to Nixon's personal reelection organization, CRP. Alternatively, they had been threatened with tax audits by the Internal Revenue Service or promised favors from the government. As a result of the "Milk Fund" disclosures, it was revealed that dairy farmers received higher price supports (government supplementary payments) for milk in exchange for contributions to the president's reelection campaign. The public also learned that White House aides had recruited men to play "dirty tricks" on Democratic candidates during the primaries. Their efforts to forge press releases and letters, disrupt candidates' schedules, and foul up telephone lines came to light, too. The American people were receiving an unexpected civics lesson.

The hearings attracted a nationwide television audience, and when public television replayed the testimony at night, its ratings tripled and quadrupled. During the daytime, the Watergate hearings received higher ratings than the soap operas that usually dominate the network schedules.[8] It wasn't until late in September that the broadcasters resumed their normal programming and Watergate left the airwaves. The committee itself continued to meet until July 1974 when it released its final report, having spent $1.5 million of the taxpayers' money on the proceedings. One measurement of the hearings' impact could be seen in the president's approval ratings. According to the Gallup poll, in February 1973 the public had given him a 68 percent positive rating. By July, it had slipped to 40 percent.[9]

Besides the Watergate Committee hearings, another Watergate investigation was making headlines. A new special prosecutor began presenting witnesses to the Watergate grand jury. (Special prosecutors are private, independent lawyers appointed to handle especially controversial cases that are seen as "hot potatoes.") Because these attorneys are outsiders, they are expected to handle these cases more impartially than the government's legal staff. Many times before, Nixon had rejected proposals to bring a special prosecutor into the Watergate case. He preferred the tactic of telling partial truths in the hope the scandal would blow over. When Elliot Richardson was offered the post of attorney general, the president gave him the option of naming a special prosecutor. Richardson soon announced the appointment of an independent counsel, citing his own previous service under Nixon in several cabinet-level positions as the reason.

On May 18, Attorney General Richardson named Archibald Cox to the post of special prosecutor. Tall and lanky, with a gray crew cut, Archibald Cox had been one of Richardson's professors at Harvard Law School. Cox had a reputation as a righteous and inflexible Yankee, a man of the highest integrity. His close ties to the Kennedy family did not endear him to Richard Nixon, who never forgot his 1960 presidential defeat at the hands of the Kennedys.

Cox organized special task forces to look into the Watergate break-in and cover-up, 1972 campaign financing, campaign "dirty tricks," and the activities of the Plumbers unit, among other things. His staff compelled the same witnesses testifying before the Watergate Committee to appear before them and provide information that might lead to further grand jury indictments. Meanwhile Cox went into action. He almost made an enemy of a potential ally when he insisted that the Senate committee call off its public hearings because these might deny participants in the Watergate cover-up a fair trial. The request was denied. Then, on July 23, his office antagonized the White House by issuing subpoenas for nine specific tapes, all related to the Watergate affair. When the president's counsel Fred Buzhardt rejected the legal order, Cox took the matter to court.

Appearing before Judge John Sirica on July 26, Cox argued that the tapes were necessary as evidence in pending criminal cases. The president's lawyer, Charles Wright, recently hired from the University of Texas, based the refusal to comply on the principle of executive privilege. He argued that the president needed privacy to receive and evaluate advice from his aides in order to conduct the business of government. On August 29, the judge ordered that the tapes be turned over to him so that he might remove any sensitive portions before releasing them to the grand jury.

In September, Nixon's attorney brought the case to the Court of Appeals. There Cox and Wright reviewed the history of executive privilege. Then Wright made an important point when he argued that if the court denied Richard Nixon's claim, presidents might have to turn over confidential materials to every courtroom in the land. The judges on the Appeals Court were mostly liberals appointed by Presidents Kennedy and Johnson. However, instead of using this occasion to embarrass the current conservative Republican president, these jurists urged the warring officials of the executive branch to seek a compromise.

The judges wanted the officials to agree to an arrangement that would protect the president's privacy but give the special prosecutor the evidence he needed. In this situation, any invasion of the president's privacy would prove disastrous. Nixon simply could not allow it. So, of course, the lawyers could not reach an agreement. The case went back to court. On October 12, the judges issued a decision. Reluctantly, they upheld Judge Sirica's ruling that the president must hand over the tapes. However, they gave the president five days to take the matter to the Supreme Court or strike a compromise with Cox before complying with the court order.

The president had other matters on his mind. He was keeping an eye on the Yom Kippur War between Israel and the Arab nations abroad while faced with a very serious crisis on the home front. On October 10, his vice president Spiro Agnew resigned, rather than face a lengthy impeachment proceeding to remove him from office. The vice presidential crisis had been festering all throughout the late spring and summer. During this period, the administration learned that while Agnew was governor of Maryland and later, as vice president, he had accepted bribes from construction company executives. As governor, he had also failed to pay federal income taxes. A prolonged inquiry into another administration scandal with more bad publicity was just what the White House did not need. The sooner Agnew left office, the better. Plea bargaining, (negotiations to reduce penalties in exchange for an admission of guilt to a lesser charge), seemed the fastest solution. After Agnew resigned, he paid a fine and never went to prison.

The Agnew debacle greatly embarrassed an already

troubled administration. Immediately, Richard Nixon took steps to restore public confidence in the government. The Twenty-fifth Amendment to the Constitution permits the president to fill a vacancy in the office of vice president by nominating a replacement. The name is then submitted to both houses of Congress for their approval by a majority vote. On October 12, President Nixon announced the selection of popular House leader Representative Gerald R. Ford of Michigan for his second in command. Ford took the oath of office in December 1973 and became the nation's first unelected vice president. There the matter ended, but the ongoing problem of the Watergate tapes was still on the president's mind. On October 12, he was supposed to surrender the tapes if he failed to accept the alternatives outlined by the Court of Appeals.

Richard Nixon had already chosen an altogether different solution. In an attempt to outmaneuver the judges, he had shrewdly ordered his staff to prepare a summary of the nine subpoenaed conversations. Archibald Cox was to reject this alternative. Attorney General Richardson let it be known that if Cox were to be fired for refusing to accept Nixon's version of the subpoenaed tapes, he would leave his post as head of the Justice Department. Richardson had promised that the special prosecutor would have the freedom to conduct an independent inquiry into the Watergate affair, which is what Archibald Cox was trying to do. However, the president was firm in his determination to keep the actual tapes, and the prosecutor was equally insistent that he needed them. A clash was inevitable.

Meanwhile, on October 17, Judge Sirica rejected the Senate committee chairman Sam Ervin's request for the tapes on grounds of executive privilege. The Watergate Committee was part of a rival branch of government.

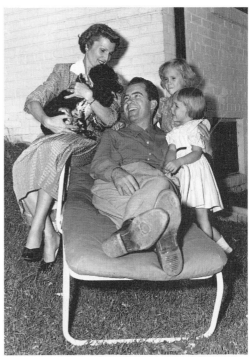

Richard M. Nixon as a three-year-old boy (top left, at extreme right) in a family portrait; relaxing with his wife, Pat, daughters Patricia and Julie, and their dog Checkers in 1952 (top right); and in the Oval Office.

The Democratic National Committee headquarters was
housed in the sprawling Watergate complex.

Ex-FBI agent G. Gordon Liddy (center), the flamboyant chief of the Plumbers unit who masterminded the Watergate operation, and six of the seven men convicted for the break-in (clockwise from top left): Howard Hunt, James McCord, Jr., Frank Sturgis, Virgilio Gonzalez, Eugenio Martinez, and Bernard Barker. Liddy served over four years in prison—the longest Watergate sentence. Co-ringleader Hunt served thirty-three months, and the five burglars served prison terms ranging from thirteen to fifteen months.

Washington Post *reporters Bob Woodward
(left) and Carl Bernstein relentlessly
investigated the Watergate case.*

In the spring of 1973, the president appeared on nation-wide television, announcing that he was assuming "full responsibility" for the Watergate inquiry.

Attorney General Richard Kleindienst (right) and three of Nixon's trusted aides (below left to right), John Ehrlichman, H. R. Haldeman, and John Dean, were swept out of office by the Watergate bugging scandal.

Chief District Court
Judge John Sirica

Senator Sam Ervin
(left), chairman
of the Senate
Watergate Committee,
holds up several
checks that were
allegedly secretly
cashed and used to
fund the Watergate
operation.

Fired White House counsel John Dean testifies before the Senate Watergate Committee (his wife is seated behind him). During his testimony, he presented two letters (below), which he said were written by President Nixon. Dean told the committee that upon reading the letters of resignation and request for leave of absence he told the president he could not sign them.

THE WHITE HOUSE
WASHINGTON

April 16, 1973

DESK COPY

Dear Mr. President:

You have informed me that Bob Haldeman and John Ehrlichman have verbally tendered their requests to be given an immediate and indefinite leave of absence from your staff. By this letter I also wish to confirm my similar request that I be given such a leave of absence from the staff.

Sincerely, DESK COPY
Do Not Remove
From Senate Press Gallery

John W. Dean, III
Counsel to the President

Honorable Richard Nixon
The President of the United States
The White House
Washington, D. C. 20500

THE WHITE HOUSE
WASHINGTON

April 16, 1973

Dear Mr. President:

As a result of my involvement in the Watergate matter, which we discussed last night and today, I tender to you my resignation effective at once.

Sincerely,

The President
The White House
Washington, D. C.

*H. R. Haldeman gives his testimony to
the Senate Watergate Committee.*

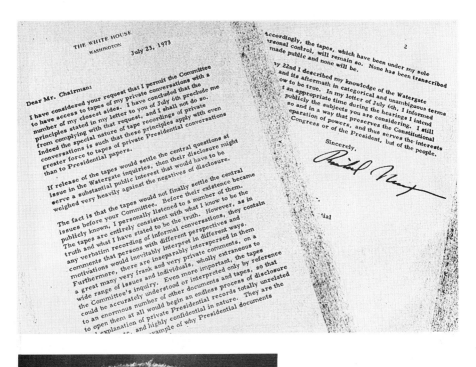

Nixon sent Senator Ervin a letter (above) in which he refused to give up recordings of his taped conversations with his former aides. The letter apparently did not daunt Special Prosecutor Archibald Cox (left), who said he was confident Nixon would surrender the tapes if the Supreme Court ordered him to do so.

(Top) The "Saturday Night Massacre": Press Secretary
Ronald Ziegler announces the resignation of Attorney General
Elliot Richardson and the dismissal of Archibald Cox. (Bottom)
With copies of the White House transcripts prominently
displayed on national television, the president announced he
was releasing edited transcripts of the Watergate tapes.

This sketch shows Nixon's attorney James St. Clair arguing before the Supreme Court over whether President Nixon could assert executive privilege in withholding the tapes demanded as evidence by Special Prosecutor Leon Jaworski (left).

Editorial cartoonists had a field day with the Watergate scandal.

Members of the Committee to Impeach the President demonstrate in front of the White House.

The House Judiciary Committee (top) voted 27–11 to recommend the impeachment of President Nixon for obstruction of justice in the Watergate cover-up.

Nixon speaks with Secretary of State Henry Kissinger and Secretary of Defense James Schlesinger during a cabinet meeting held two days before the president announced his resignation (below), on August 8, 1974.

The president bids an
emotional farewell
to members of his
staff, and embraces
his daughter Julie
at the White House.

Nixon flashes the victory sign before boarding
a helicopter bound for California, where he
would begin life as a private citizen.

Unlike the Special Prosecutor's office, a division of the executive branch, it did not require the tapes as evidence in criminal cases. Sirica reasoned that the purpose of executive privilege was to let a president withhold certain private matters from congressional scrutiny.

In a public statement on October 19, the president presented himself as a concerned but reasonable man. He declared his intention to cooperate with the courts and the Senate. Hoping to improve his image in Congress, Richard Nixon offered to make summaries of the tapes available to the much respected senator John Stennis of Mississippi. This Democratic lawmaker would check them for accuracy before they were released. It was not generally known that Stennis was partially deaf, and that the tape recordings were quite fuzzy. There were so many background noises that it was sometimes hard to hear what was being said. The president announced that chairman Sam Ervin and vice chairman Howard Baker had agreed to the proposal. It made sense for the two men to accept the president's offer once the courts had otherwise made the tapes inaccessible to them. The president went on to state that he had directed Archibald Cox, as an employee of the executive branch, to stop trying to get the tapes. In effect, Nixon was giving Cox one last chance to keep his job. In his announcement, Richard Nixon had neglected to mention the fact that what he was doing did not comply with the Court of Appeals' decision. The court had ordered him to surrender copies of the actual tapes, but the president chose to release summaries of the tapes' contents instead.

A defiant Cox responded to the presidential order by telling reporters that Nixon's directive violated his independence as special prosecutor and undermined his position. Cox called a press conference and explained:

I am certainly not out to get the president of the United States. I am even worried, to put it in colloquial terms, that I am getting too big for my britches, that what I see as principle could be vanity. I hope not. In the end I had to stick by what I thought was right. [10]

During the question-and-answer session with reporters, Cox pointed out that the ground rules he agreed upon when he took on the job of special prosecutor had been changed. He found the change unacceptable because it prevented him from doing his job. Replying to a reporter's question about whether he would follow the president's orders, Cox stated that since the attorney general had hired him, the attorney general was the only official Cox was legally obligated to obey.

The president was infuriated. He directed the attorney general to fire Cox. Elliot Richardson did not obey this presidential order. He had made a commitment to Cox that the special prosecutor would only be fired for extraordinary misconduct. Cox had acted diligently and conscientiously. So, Richardson resigned instead of carrying out an unacceptable order. His deputy William Ruckelshaus, next in command, made a similar decision. That left Robert Bork, the solicitor general, to dismiss Cox. (The solicitor general is the official who argues the government's cases before the Supreme Court and gives approval to government requests to appeal a case to a higher court.) Bork decided that, despite his personal distaste for the job, he would do what the president wanted done. On Saturday night, October 20, presidential press secretary Ron Ziegler announced the resignations and dismissal and told reporters that the office of special prosecutor had been abolished.

The Saturday Night Massacre, as the media called it, brought a spontaneous and angry outburst from the public. Most thought that the president was wrong to fire Cox.

They believed that Nixon overestimated his power when he refused to give the courts the evidence the law required. No longer was the Watergate break-in or the cover-up the object of their concern. Some protestors held up signs for cars to "Honk for Impeachment." Two of the major networks devoted news specials to the event. Then the White House was deluged with letters criticizing the president's actions. Republican as well as Democratic political leaders expressed their indignation. Deans from seventeen law schools urged Congress to consider impeaching the president. The president was stunned by the uproar he had created. He had never expected this reaction.

To make amends, on October 23, a weary Richard Nixon agreed to release the nine tapes Cox originally requested. However, there was a hitch in this display of presidential good will. Two of the subpoenaed tapes did not exist. The taping system had not recorded the contents of a phone conversation John Mitchell had had with the president. Neither could the White House supply a tape of John Dean's talk with Richard Nixon on April 15. The Dictabelt machine had been left unattended and ran out of tape. When Nixon had learned about the missing April 15th tape, he suggested to Fred Buzhardt that they manufacture a new one. The horrified attorney discouraged the desperate president from taking such an unlawful action. It had become obvious that the president had little respect for the law and would do anything to obstruct ongoing legal proceedings. When the public learned about the missing tapes, they were outraged.

On November 1, with his popular approval rating at an all-time low, the president tried to cut his losses. He announced the appointment of a new attorney general, William Saxbe, and a new special prosecutor, Leon Jaworski. Jaworski accepted this difficult post because Chief of Staff Alexander Haig promised him that he would be completely independent of the president and could even take the president to court, if necessary. Jaworski, a Democrat who had studied law at Baylor and George Washington University, had an impressive background. He had been a prosecutor in the Nuremberg war crimes trials at the conclusion of World War II and was president of the American Bar Association from 1971 to 1972. Unlike the scholarly Cox, Jaworski was a practical man, accustomed to the give-and-take of politics.

Jaworski retained most of Cox's investigating team and went to work. Following Cox's thwarted plans, he requested other tapes from the White House, including ones concerning the Plumbers unit. Then Jaworski received a visit from presidential lawyer Fred Buzhardt, who told the surprised special prosecutor that one of the original nine subpoenaed Watergate tapes, Nixon's conversation with H. R. Haldeman on June 20, had a rather large gap in it, a gap of eighteen and a half minutes. However, Buzhardt did have Haldeman's notes on the meeting and related their contents to Jaworski. The president's lawyer claimed that the gap probably occurred when Nixon's private secretary, Rose Mary Woods, was transcribing the tapes. The media released the story on November 21. The public was justifiably enraged when it got wind of this latest gaffe.

When Judge Sirica was informed about the gap, he decided to call for a hearing and selected a panel of experts to examine the suspect tape. Ms. Woods told the judge that General Haig had instructed her not to transcribe this conversation between Haldeman and the president because it had not been subpoenaed. However, at one time when she was listening to the Haldeman-Nixon tape she was interrupted by a five-minute phone call. Afterward, she discovered that she had pushed the record button instead of the stop button. She played back the tape. Part of the conversation had been lost. She told the president about her mistake, and he reassured her that the conversation had not been subpoenaed. Buzhardt and other White House aides told Judge Sirica that they, too, had not thought the tape had been subpoenaed. It was not until later that they learned it was needed as evidence. Then they listened to it and found the gap. Judge Sirica's experts eventually concluded that the gap was the result of a deliberate erasure. The erasure involved from five to nine separate operations at the controls of Ms. Woods's transcribing machine. The culprit was never found.

On November 17, Richard Nixon appeared before several hundred newspaper editors for a televised question-and-answer session. He still hoped to improve his image with the public. The media gave wide coverage to a statement he made during that meeting.

> *In all my years of public life, I have never obstructed justice. And, I think, too, that I could say that in my years of public life, that I welcome this kind of examination, because people have got to know whether or not their President is a crook. Well, I am not a crook.* [11]

Those who had worked with the president in the past and even some of his more recent appointees could no longer accept his statement of innocence at face value. Only six weeks after accepting the post of special prosecutor, Leon Jaworski thought the president was guilty. He recommended to presidential chief of staff Alexander Haig that the president hire a good criminal lawyer. Haig reluctantly agreed. He had learned that Garment was about to return to his private practice, and the president was not getting along with Buzhardt. After Buzhardt had reviewed some of the presidential tapes and discussed them with Garment, both men privately came to the conclusion that the president had stepped outside the law. So Haig arranged to hire Bostonian James D. St. Clair, an outstanding trial lawyer. A graduate of Harvard Law School, the attorney saw this opportunity to work for the president as the chance of a lifetime. By December, there were rumblings in the House of Representatives about the possibility of impeachment proceedings, the constitutional method of removing a president from office. The Watergate scandal was far from over, and Richard Nixon would need all the help he could get.

6

THE SMOKING GUN

How to guarantee the president and his men a fair trial was the difficult problem facing Peter Rodino, chairman of the House Judiciary Committee, and Leon Jaworski, special prosecutor. In the United States, people charged with a crime—whether presidents or ordinary citizens—are entitled to have their day in court without unreasonable delay. They have the right to compel witnesses to testify for them and to obtain materials necessary for their defense. Because the burden of proof rests with the accuser, not the accused, Americans cannot be forced to make damaging statements against themselves. These principles are spelled out in the Bill of Rights.

It would be difficult enough for the congressman and the special prosecutor to bring the president and his men to justice. However, their task was complicated because the president refused to give them tapes of his conversations about the Watergate cover-up and other illegal activities. After the Saturday Night Massacre, Richard Nixon had reluctantly handed over seven tapes, but there were many more. The additional tapes were vital in determining, once and for all, what the president's men had done.

The tapes would finally reveal what the president knew and when he knew it.

On October 30, 1973, after the dramatic firing of so many members of the Department of Justice, the House Judiciary Committee began to consider the possibility of impeaching Richard Nixon, removing him from office. However, it was not until February 6, 1974, that the House of Representatives actually voted 410–4 to start the proceedings and gave its Judiciary Committee broad subpoena powers. According to the Constitution, the House of Representatives, upon the recommendation of its Judiciary Committee, has the power to vote formal charges, articles of impeachment, against the president. These are equivalent to a grand jury indictment. Then the president is tried before the Senate and found guilty or acquitted.

House Judiciary Committee chairman, sixty-four-year-old Peter Rodino, was a pleasant, grandfatherly man with a round face framed by hair that was beginning to turn white. A Democrat from New Jersey, he had served in the House for twenty-five years, representing an Italian-American district. Rodino had not achieved much public recognition during his years of service, but he had won the respect of his colleagues. Yet, some congressmen wondered whether he would have the drive needed to handle a presidential impeachment. House Speaker and Democratic leader Carl Albert defended his choice, saying, "Pete is not the most aggressive member in the House. He's a little bit shy, but he runs a smooth, complete shop. I didn't want to go with one of the more spectacular members of the House or someone who wanted to be a movie star."[1] Quietly, Rodino presided over twenty-one Democrats and seventeen Republicans, a cross section of men and women, blacks and whites. All of them were lawyers.

The committee's first task was to hire a staff. Rodino chose John Doar as counsel, legal advisor to the committee. A man in his early fifties, Republican Doar had a reputation for personal integrity. He was not an expert in constitutional law, but he was a hard, solid worker. These were the qualities Rodino wanted. The two men were set on holding an impartial inquiry into the facts and refused to hire staff who expressed any opinion whatsoever about the president. Privately, Rodino and Doar suspected that Richard Nixon had violated his oath of office by abusing his powers. Now they would try to prove it as objectively as possible.

The president was not going to be impeached because he had used "dirty tricks" to defeat George McGovern. He would not be accused by a mere group of vindictive Democrats. Nor would he be defended just by devoted Republicans on the grounds that the Democrats were out to get him. What Nixon might have done was a matter of concern to all Americans. That is why the Judiciary staff's headquarters in the Congressional Hotel was placed under tight security. There would be no leaks to the media, no premature disclosures of the case against the president. The staff settled down and started to gather the facts it needed.

On February 14, two men began to present their opposing views on impeachment. John Doar, the committee's legal counsel, and James St. Clair, the president's lawyer, were evenly matched. Tall and curly haired, Doar had headed the Civil Rights Division of the Justice Department during the Kennedy and Johnson administrations. St. Clair, a stocky man, had gotten his start as an aide to Joseph Welch, helping to defend the U.S. Army against communist-baiting Joseph McCarthy's infamous charges during Senate hearings in the 1950s.

Each side had searched through history to support its interpretation of what "high crimes and misdemeanors" meant. This ambiguous phrase is the constitutional basis for impeaching a president. The staffs studied the English Civil Wars of the 1640s and debates at the American

Constitutional Convention. However, these sources offered confused and contradictory guidelines. The only historical example of presidential impeachment they had was the case of Andrew Johnson. It was not very helpful since Johnson, unlike Richard Nixon, had been charged with violating an act of Congress.

Eventually Doar and his staff took the position that the president himself does not have to commit a criminal act to be removed from office. All that is needed is proof of substantial misconduct. From the committee's point of view, impeachment was a remedy to keep government within constitutional limits, rather than a personal punishment for a president. James St. Clair presented the Judiciary Committee with a counterargument. He insisted that a president could be impeached only if he was accused of a specific crime. In the absence of such a charge, it would be impossible to remove him from office nor could his lawyers defend him.

At the conclusion of the debate, the committee had still failed to define exactly what they meant by an impeachable offense. As the chairman and the head of his committee staff knew, they still lacked hard evidence that the president's role in the cover-up was an unlawful act— despite all the material they had reviewed from the Ervin committee, the grand jury investigation, and the president's statements. Rodino and his committee desperately needed to establish the facts. They had to find out if indeed laws had been violated. Then they could decide whether or not to bring charges.

Meanwhile, special prosecutor Leon Jaworski and the Watergate grand jury were gathering evidence to bring charges against the president's men. Jaworski and his staff studied the seven tapes Nixon had released after the Saturday Night Massacre and heard what some of the White House aides had said about their participation in the cover-up. What was needed was proof of their "corrupt intent," proof that they had deliberately set out to violate the law. That proof would be hard to get. In conversations with the president's chief of staff, Alexander Haig, and in correspondence with lawyer James St. Clair, Jaworski learned that Nixon was not prepared to release any more tapes.

From the evidence he had already obtained about the Watergate cover-up, Jaworski was convinced that the president, too, was guilty of criminal misconduct. However, it would be almost impossible to indict an office-holding president unless he had committed a capital crime, such as murder. So, the special prosecutor came up with an alternative plan. By January 7, Jaworski and his staff prepared a detailed document of what the president had done. They kept all eight copies of it under tightest security. It became the basis for an unprecedented act.

Citing examples of the president's misconduct, Jaworski asked the grand jury to name President Nixon an unindicted coconspirator in the Watergate cover-up. This meant that the court would officially recognize that the president had taken part in the cover-up conspiracy, but no formal charges would be brought against him. It had never been done before in the history of American jurisprudence. However, Jaworski was ready to break precedent in order to make the president's taped statements admissible as evidence in the upcoming trial of his advisors. To use the tapes, rules of evidence required that the president be named as part of the cover-up conspiracy before the Watergate trial took place. Both the prosecution and the defense wanted access to additional tapes to strengthen their cases. Now they would have grounds to subpoena them.

The special prosecutor had decided not to ask the grand jury to bring charges against the president in open court. If the charges were made, the actual indictment process could drag on for months, making it difficult for the chief executive to govern effectively. The indictment would receive so much publicity that the president would be denied his constitutional rights. This is why the special prosecutor pledged the grand jury to secrecy for the time being. He also wanted to make sure that the president got a fair hearing before the House Judiciary Committee. Accordingly, the grand jurors sent a confidential report to the court, giving the facts of the president's role in the cover-up and naming him as an unindicted coconspirator. With Judge Sirica's approval, one copy of the report—without mention of the president's legal status—was sent to the Judiciary Committee. The others were locked in a safe.

The committee members had been having difficulty rounding up the evidence they needed so Peter Rodino and his staff welcomed the edited report from Judge Sirica's court. They were grateful for the enclosed tapes of the president's conversation on March 21 with his advisors. His comments about paying blackmail to Howard Hunt gave them proof that the president had actually committed a crime. Now they could point to a specific impeachable offense, but they did not do so yet.

To make their case airtight, they wanted still more tapes. On April 11, the House Judiciary Committee subpoenaed copies of forty-two taped conversations from the White House, giving the president until April 30 to hand them over. Nixon decided to stall for time, rather than release the damaging materials at once. He reasoned that since the committee had not yet told him how they defined an impeachable offense, it would be impossible for him to supply the material they needed. He felt they were merely off on a "fishing expedition," and he refused to bait their hook.

On March 1, John Mitchell, H. R. Haldeman, John

Ehrlichman, Charles Colson, and three other aides were formally indicted as participants in the Watergate cover-up. They were charged with a conspiracy to obstruct justice and with perjury. Then, on March 7, Ehrlichman, Colson, and five others were also indicted for their involvement in the break-in at the office of Daniel Ellsberg's psychiatrist. From conversations with Haig, Jaworski concluded that Haldeman and Ehrlichman would plead innocent to the Watergate charges to avoid implicating the president. The special prosecutor expected that the president would be more willing to turn over the tapes now that they might help clear his advisors as well as himself. However, the president did not act as Jaworski had anticipated. Instead, Nixon planned to review the tapes. He would give up only those excerpts that strengthened his own position and that made John Dean's earlier testimony look bad. On April 18, faced with continued White House delays, Jaworski went back to court and got Judge Sirica to issue a subpoena for sixty-four conversations related to the cover-up and other matters under investigation.

On April 29, just one day before he had to respond to the Judiciary Committee subpoena for forty-two tapes, Richard Nixon went on nationwide television. With great fanfare, he announced that he was releasing edited transcripts of thirty-one of the forty-two tapes and seven others. The television camera focused on a table in the Oval Office stacked with impressive gold-embossed binders containing the transcripts. Actually, some of the binders were empty because the president's staff had not yet finished preparing all the documents. Here was striking proof of the president's belief that appearances mattered more than reality. The speech itself as well as the release of the edited conversations were designed to keep up appearances.

From his desk in the Oval Office, Nixon described the

private talks as "strategy sessions, the exploration of alternatives, the weighing of human and political costs."[2] He explained that he was making these transcripts of his discussions public because impeachment was an ordeal that would "be felt throughout the world, and it would have its effect on the lives of all Americans for many years to come."[3] The president insisted that he had "nothing to hide." He said that the transcripts "will at last once and for all show that what I knew and what I did with regard to the Watergate break-in and cover-up were just as I have described them to you from the beginning. . . . In giving these—blemishes and all—I am placing my trust in the basic fairness of the American people."[4]

The blemishes the president referred to could not be covered up with public relations cosmetics. His staff had carefully edited the transcripts to remove incriminating statements and to cut out coarse language. They substituted the words "expletive deleted" for some of the president's cruder expressions. However, release of the transcripts proved very embarrassing to the president. His language made him seem to be "cynical, petty, and self-ish."[5] Even with the expletives deleted, his use of profanity, ethnic slurs, and vulgarity could easily be inferred. The contrast between these personal, private comments and his dignified official statements was so sharp that the public was shocked. For many, his choice of language may have been even more offensive than his actual suggestions about the cover-up. Within two weeks, a Harris poll revealed that 49 percent of the public favored Nixon's impeachment. Earlier, in April, before the transcripts were released, only 17 percent had supported impeachment.[6]

The president had thought he could hide some of the damaging material he had been ordered to hand over by burying it in over 1,200 pages of edited transcripts. The press plowed through the 200,000 or more words and quickly made headlines out of such presidential comments as "hanging in tough," "stonewall it," and "keep the cap on the bottle." On May 1, the Judiciary Committee voted 20–18, along party lines, that the transcripts did not meet the subpoena's demand for copies of the actual taped conversations.

On May 8, after months of investigation by the committee staff, Chairman Rodino opened formal hearings on the impeachment of President Nixon. (Public hearings would not be held until July.) Following a brief debate, House Judiciary Committee members voted 31–6 to consider the evidence they had gathered behind closed doors. The event, broadcast live on nationwide television, took just twenty minutes. Then James St. Clair was permitted to listen as John Doar droned on and on, reading from the two thick volumes of evidence that had been placed on the desk of every committee member. Both Doar and Rodino had carefully planned to keep their own conclusions from the committee in the hope that the contents of the two volumes alone would be sufficient to convince twenty-one Democrats and six or more Republicans to impeach the president by a nonpartisan majority. Among the president's strongest defenders were Republicans Charles W. Sandman, Jr. of New Jersey and Charles Wiggins of California. Democrat Paul Sarbanes of Maryland was equally determined to bring the president to justice. Between these two extremes lay the "swing votes," members of Congress whose minds were not firmly made up. These were the people Rodino and Doar sought to convince.

Like the Judiciary Committee, the special prosecutor's office was dissatisfied with the new set of edited transcripts. Leon Jaworski found them a poor substitute for the sixty-four conversations he had subpoenaed. Ever a shrewd bargainer, Jaworski met with Chief of Staff Alexander Haig. He told the astonished presidential advisor that

Richard Nixon had already been named an unindicted coconspirator in the Watergate cover-up. Jaworski was hoping to strike a deal with Haig to secure the eighteen most important tapes he had subpoenaed. In exchange, the special prosecutor would continue to keep the president's status as an unindicted co-conspirator a secret and possibly strike it from the record. Jaworski explained to the chief of staff that he had hoped the Judiciary Committee's hearings would be over before he released the damaging grand jury report, but the date of the trial of the Watergate defendants, Haldeman, Ehrlichman, Mitchell, and others, was drawing near. At that point, the sensational news would be announced. When Haig duly reported this conversation to Nixon, the president refused to give in to pressure and turned down the special prosecutor's offer. He would go ahead with his efforts to block Jaworski's efforts to get the tapes.

At the inevitable court hearing, presidential lawyer James St. Clair claimed that the special prosecutor had no right to demand the tapes because he was a member of the executive branch. Members of the executive branch could not sue one another. Jaworski argued that according to the terms of his appointment, he was given the authority to take the president to court, if necessary. The Senate Judiciary Committee passed a resolution backing Jaworski's stand. Finally, Judge Sirica ruled that the special prosecutor was entitled to the tapes. During the hearing, someone told the press that Nixon had been named an unindicted co-conspirator, and Jaworski's carefully kept secret became the subject of banner headlines.

Aware that the subpoenaed tapes would destroy his presidency, Nixon refused to surrender them. His lawyer James St. Clair went to the Court of Appeals to seek a reversal of Judge Sirica's ruling. Leon Jaworski feared that the entire appeals process would take so long that the trial of the Watergate defendants, originally scheduled for September 9, might have to be postponed until 1975. Then the defendants could claim that they had been denied their constitutional right to a speedy trial. With this in mind, on May 24, Jaworski decided to take an unusual step. He appealed directly to the Supreme Court for a ruling on his subpoena for the tapes.

When a case is of "imperative public importance," the Supreme Court will sometimes agree to hear it directly—bypassing the Court of Appeals. Although the justices were under pressure to decide a number of important cases before they adjourned for the summer, they agreed to hear this case. Justice William Rehnquist disqualified himself because he had previously served in the Justice Department under Attorney General John Mitchell.

During the month of June, the troubled president took off for foreign lands. He traveled to the Middle East, then headed for the Soviet Union and a summit meeting with Leonid I. Brezhnev. In the past, his personal diplomacy had always won favor with the public. Perhaps the trips would bring him some positive results and restore his sagging prestige. While the president was abroad, some of his aides, who had pleaded guilty to the charges against them, received prison sentences and fines for their role in trying to discredit Daniel Ellsberg and for their participation in the Watergate cover-up.

On July 8, the lawyers for each side came to present their arguments at the Supreme Court. They were surprised by the large crowds they had attracted. What caught Jaworski's attention was the number of young people with sleeping bags who had camped out near the steps of the Supreme Court building in the hope of witnessing history in the making.[7] Inside, a hush came over the spectators as the marshal called for order. Then the eight black-robed justices entered the chamber and took their places on the bench. Lawyers for each side stood ready to present their arguments in *United States* v. *Nixon.*

Jaworski opened with the claim that the tapes were needed as evidence in a criminal trial and that the president was withholding them to hide his own wrongdoing. By invoking executive privilege, the president was offering his own interpretation of the Constitution to defend his right to keep the tapes. The special prosecutor posed the question: Who is the ultimate interpreter of the law, the president or the Supreme Court? When it was St. Clair's turn, the president's lawyer insisted that the Court had no right to hear the case since it was a matter of politics, not law. Further, he argued that the doctrine of executive privilege gave the president the exclusive right to determine what should be released and what should not.

On July 9, Peter Rodino decided to make public the Judiciary Committee's version of eight original Watergate tapes the committee possessed. With superior electronic equipment, the committee staff was able to point up significant differences between the presidential and the committee versions in side-by-side comparisons of text. The transcripts the president had supplied came in a poor second. This had led Rodino to personally conclude that the cover-up was still going on. The president's lawyer tried to explain away the original omissions, and press secretary Ron Ziegler dismissed the whole affair as a partisan public relations campaign.

On July 11, John Dean arrived to testify before a closed session of the Judiciary Committee. St. Clair tried to discredit his story that the president had given permission for $75,000 to be paid to Hunt as blackmail. The president's lawyer claimed that Dean had told the Senate Watergate Committee the matter had been left undecided. Dean explained to the mortified attorney that there had been two discussions about money, one about Hunt and one about paying off all the burglars. Only the latter had been left undecided. Throughout the rest of his cross-examination, St. Clair was not able to triumph over Dean. As a former participant in the cover-up, Dean was far better informed than the president's lawyer. The president had not confided in St. Clair, nor did he let him in on all the damaging evidence the tapes contained.

On July 18, James St. Clair presented his final arguments before the House Judiciary Committee. He kept to the position he had held since the closed hearings began. Impeachment could only be justified by "clear and convincing" evidence "[b]ecause anything less than that, in my view, is going to result in recrimination, bitterness, and divisiveness among our people."[8] The lawyer submitted a new transcript he had just received from the president, an excerpt from a conversation between Haldeman and Nixon the day after the Dean discussion about hush money for Hunt had taken place. In this discussion, the president claimed that he did not intend to be blackmailed by Hunt.

Over objections from committee members about the last-minute submission of evidence, Chairman Rodino let St. Clair continue to defend the president. Rodino was willing to bend over backwards to be fair to the president. When the lawyer concluded, new protests arose. The transcript was about two pages long while the original conversation, still under subpoena, had lasted for almost an hour and a half. The chairman calmly dismissed the lawyer. He had long since recognized that St. Clair did not have the president's confidence and was merely being used to mouth to the committee what the president wanted him to say. The next day Doar presented the case for impeachment. He stated:

What he [the president] decided should be done following the Watergate break-in caused action not only by his own servants, but by the agencies of the United

States, including the Department of Justice, the FBI,
the CIA, and the Secret Service. It required perjury,
destruction of evidence, obstruction of justice, all
crimes. But, most important of all, it required deliber-
ate, contrived, continued, and continuing deception of
the American people. 9

On July 23, the day before the Judiciary Committee had
scheduled its long-postponed public hearings, the Supreme Court issued a ruling in the case of *United States v.*
Nixon. The impressive chamber with its dark red carpets
and double rows of tall marble pillars was jammed with
spectators and reporters. White porcelain rosettes high up
on the ceiling illuminated the tense audience. Chief Justice Warren Burger, seated in his black leather chair, spoke
a few words in memory of the man he succeeded, former
chief justice Earl Warren, who had recently died. Then he
leaned forward and read the unanimous decision of the
Court on the president's claim to executive privilege. The
justices reasoned as follows: First, the special prosecutor
had the right to bring the case to the Court, even though
it was a dispute between members of the executive branch.
The attorney general had given the special prosecutor the
authority to do this and had not seen fit to revoke that
authority. Second, the preliminary hearings had shown
that the tapes contained evidence vital to a pending criminal trial. Third, and most important, the Court judged
that while the president certainly has the right to keep his
conversations with subordinates confidential, he exercises
a limited, not an absolute, right to executive privilege. It
is the duty of the Supreme Court, not the president, to
determine what the law is. In this case, it was necessary
that the tapes be used in a criminal trial. 10

The news was quickly relayed to the president. He was
furious. He fumed that he had appointed Burger, Black-

mun, and Powell to the court. How could they not support him? Like many presidents before him, Richard Nixon expected gratitude from the men he appointed to the bench, and like many other presidents, he was disappointed. The Supreme Court justices had risen above politics, or at least, Richard Nixon's brand of politics. They were members of an independent judiciary, as guaranteed by the Constitution.

Among the subpoenaed tapes the Supreme Court ordered released was the fatal June 23 conversation. In this talk with Haldeman, the president had suggested that the CIA be called in to block the FBI's investigation of the Watergate break-in. When the president's aides replayed this tape, they knew that Richard Nixon was in very serious trouble. His lawyers Frederick Buzhardt and James St. Clair advised him to hand over the tapes. Initially, he resisted. Once more, the president would take his time before he chose to cooperate.

While Nixon was deciding on his next move, the House Judiciary Committee began holding its public hearings. On July 24, approximately 60 million viewers watched as television cameras swept Room 2141 of the House of Representatives. They saw a long curved bench, two rows deep. The older committee members sat in the back while the newer members had seats in the front row. Before the representatives were tables with lawyers and staff members. Spectators were crammed into chairs behind the tables. Each of the committee members had fifteen minutes to express an opinion about the issues.

Rodino spoke first, setting the tone of the proceedings by saying, "Make no mistake about it. This is a turning point, whatever we decide. Our judgment is not concerned with an individual but with a system of constitutional government."[11] No one watching the hearings would ever forget a golden-tongued representative from

Texas, Congresswoman Barbara Jordan, as she accused the president of abusing his official powers. Nor would they forget Californian Charles Wiggins's booming voice as he defended Richard Nixon.

As Rodino had hoped, over the last few weeks, a bipartisan majority for impeachment had finally taken shape. On July 27, committee members voted 27–11 in favor of the first article of impeachment against Richard Nixon. They charged him with obstructing justice by preventing a thorough investigation of the Watergate break-in and covering up other illegal activities. On July 29, they passed a second article of impeachment by a vote of 28–10. They accused the president of abusing the powers of his office to violate the rights of American citizens. On July 30, in a 21–17 decision, they indicted the president for failing to satisfy their subpoenas. However, two other articles of impeachment were voted down. By a vote of 26–12, they rejected one article condemning him for the secret bombing of Cambodia and another accusing him of tax fraud and the transfer of federal funds for use on his private homes. Just after eleven at night, Chairman Rodino closed the meeting.

Debate on the floor of the House was to begin in two weeks, after the Judiciary Committee had completed its final report. The president still hoped that he could escape an impeachment vote by the whole House. Meanwhile influential Senate leaders such as Barry Goldwater of Arizona, Robert Dole of Kansas, and John Tower of Texas were beginning to think that the president should be removed from office. House Judiciary Committee member Republican Charles Wiggins of California was still willing to undertake a floor fight to save the president until he was invited to discuss the matter with Haig and St. Clair. When he was shown a transcript of the June 23rd tape being prepared for release, the congressman realized that the president's cause was lost.

The June 23rd transcript quickly became known as the smoking gun, referring to the fact that smoke is evidence that a gun has been fired. This transcript offered conclusive evidence that the president had been a party to the conspiracy to cover up the Watergate break-in almost from the beginning. It undermined Nixon's public statements that he had known nothing about the cover-up until his conversation on March 21 with John Dean. The transcript also revealed that the president was willing to obstruct justice by calling in the CIA to block the FBI's probe of the burglary.

Senator Robert Griffin of Michigan, another loyal Nixon supporter, was also briefed about the damage the smoking gun would do. Griffin drafted a strong letter to the president urging his resignation. When faced with demands that he resign from office, Richard Nixon's immediate response was to carry the fight to the Senate and defend his presidency. However, when repeatedly told of the defection of his supporters, the president reluctantly agreed to hand over the tapes. On August 5, three new transcripts were made public, including his conversation of June 23.

In his statement accompanying the tapes, the president tried to explain away his incomplete admission on May 22, 1973, that he ordered Haldeman to call in the CIA to prevent the FBI from fully investigating the break-in. At that time, he had offered the excuse that he feared the FBI might reveal some secret CIA activities. Blaming this earlier statement on a faulty memory, he now conceded, "The June 23 tapes clearly show, however, that at the time I gave those instructions I also discussed the political aspects of the situation, and that I was aware of the advantages this course of action would have with respect to limiting possible public exposure of involvement by persons connected with the reelection committee."[12] The president stated the facts but expressed no guilt or remorse for what he had done. It was a posture he has maintained to this day.

The president also confessed that he had not informed his legal staff or the Judiciary Committee of the potential problems the tapes presented. Thus he preserved the honor of James St. Clair by revealing that the president's lawyer had had to prepare a defense without having access to the damaging materials. He had withheld nothing from the courts, because his own knowledge of the president's role in the cover-up had been limited.

On August 6, in response to the new tapes, all ten of the Republicans who had voted against impeachment announced that they would support the charges in Article One. They prepared a minority report to the Judiciary Committee's findings. It was not published, however, until August 22. In it they stated:

> We know that it has been said—and perhaps some will continue to say—that Richard Nixon was "hounded from office" by his political opponents and media critics.
>
> We feel constrained to point out, however, that it was Richard Nixon who impeded the FBI's investigation of the Watergate affair by wrongfully attempting to implicate the CIA. . . .[13]

It looked like Richard Nixon would not be able to muster much support in a fight to save his presidency on the floor of the House of Representatives. At the same time, in the event that the full House voted to sustain the charges against him, the Senate was going ahead with plans for the trial.

7

THE END TO IT

Faced with a constitutional crisis of his own making, Richard Nixon had to consider what to do next. Many pressured him to resign; others were equally determined that he vindicate himself by putting up a fight before the House and the Senate. At this point he wavered, angry, depressed, and unable to act. He was in no condition to make decisions. At times, he sounded incoherent. It seemed as if he did not truly understand what he had done wrong or why he had landed in this terrible predicament. All he knew was that politics was a war, and his enemies had the upper hand. He was growing weary of the fight but still he was reluctant to concede defeat. His sons-in-law, David Eisenhower and Edward Cox, as well as others, became concerned for his mental health. At this point, the president chose to isolate himself from everyone except his immediate family, Chief of Staff Alexander Haig, and Press Secretary Ron Ziegler.

Under these circumstances, the chief of staff felt compelled to take on unique responsibilities in a setting that was unprecedented in American history. Behind the scenes, he set in motion the series of events that would convince President Nixon to resign. Once the smoking gun surfaced, he and most of the president's other advisors had become convinced that a fight in the Senate was hopeless, that resignation was the only honorable course the president should take. Haig's was a most difficult job. If he and the president's other advisors demanded that the president step down, their actions would smack of an attempted coup d'etat, a sudden takeover of the government. On August 1, he had called upon Vice President Gerald Ford in the hope of receiving some guidance, but Ford chose to be neutral and explained that as the president's possible successor, he could not offer advice as to what Haig or the president should do. So it was up to Haig to find a way to get the president to resign of his own free will. Meanwhile, someone had to conduct affairs of state, and that someone turned out to be Alexander Haig. He ran the government in constant consultation with Henry Kissinger, the president's former national security advisor, now secretary of state. At the same time, Haig orchestrated events so that the realities of politics would point the president in the right direction. For example, he "was encouraging old friends of the President who stood by him in difficult times to tell him frankly about the prospects in Congress."[1]

On August 6, the president still had not made up his mind. However, he did manage to hold a cabinet meeting, his last cabinet meeting as things turned out. He seemed to be fighting for his political life. In rambling statements to the assembled department heads, he expressed his determination to fight. However, he was met with stony silence. Finally his attorney general suggested that he wait a week and see if he had enough support to govern effectively. When the meeting broke up, the officials carried the president's message back to their own staffs; the president was prepared to stay in office.

Then Richard Nixon hesitated again. Should he put

up a fight or resign from office? He met with Henry Kissinger, the man whose intellect he most admired. When asked for his opinion, Kissinger told the president that he ought to resign. Then the presidential liaisons with Congress, aides whose duty it was to report on the lawmakers' opinions and voting patterns, informed him that support on Capitol Hill was slipping away. This was the day that the ten Republicans on the Judiciary Committee switched their votes in favor of impeachment and wrote their minority report condemning the president for his conduct during the Watergate cover-up. At this stage, the president's daughter Julie was one of the few who really wanted him to carry on the fight.

On August 7, Haig notified Ford that the resignation would probably come on the ninth. With the cooperation of the chief of staff, the Ford transition team had already started to make plans for a smooth change of chief executives. By now, the president had heard from George Bush, the chairman of the Republican National Committee, the party's leader. He had written Nixon a compassionate letter urging him to resign. Bush wrote that Republican leaders felt he was hurting the party.

The clinching news came when a delegation of senators arrived to talk with Nixon in the Oval Office at five o'clock that afternoon. Prompted by Alexander Haig, Senators Barry Goldwater, influential conservative spokesman Hugh Scott, the Republican minority leader, and Representative John Rhodes, House minority leader, did not demand that the president resign. Haig was trying to prevent the president from once again feeling the need to put up a fight to defend his administration. Instead, the three leaders broke the news to him that his support in the Senate was virtually gone.

G   Mr. President, this isn't pleasant, but you want
     to know the situation and it isn't good.

P Pretty bad, huh?
G Yes, sir.
P How many would you say would be with me—
   half a dozen?
G More than that, maybe sixteen to eighteen.
P Hugh, do you agree with that?
S I'd say maybe fifteen, but it's grim, and they're
   not very firm.
P Damn grim. [2]

Around seven-thirty at night, the president made the decision to resign. He called Haig into his office to tell him. Then Nixon went back to the living quarters at the White House to join his family for dinner and share his news with them. For two hours, later that night, the president met with Henry Kissinger and discussed what went wrong over the past two years. It was a painful, emotional scene for both men. [3]

On the morning of August 8, a much-relieved Richard Nixon met with his vice president and explained to him the technical side of the resignation process. All the president had to do was write a letter giving up his post and forward it to the secretary of state. It would go into effect as soon as it was in the secretary's possession. Meanwhile, Haig had informed the White House staff of the president's resignation and arranged for Congress to be told the news. Then he set up the official meetings the president would hold that night.

Throughout the rest of the day, the president busied himself with meetings, discharging a number of personal and government business details with his aides. He found time to consider two congressional funding bills sent over to the White House for his signature before they could become law. He vetoed them, refusing his signature on the grounds that they were too costly. Once the difficult decision had been made, the president seemed more in control of himself and better able to function.

In the evening, President Nixon went over to the Executive Office building where he briefed the leaders of Congress on his decision to resign. He told them that if he fought the impeachment with a Senate trial, the procedure would take months. "It would not be fair to the country. I would be a part-time president. You would be a part-time Congress."⁴ Then he shook hands with them. His face showed the pain he felt upon parting from these old colleagues.

Then it was on to the Cabinet Room of the White House where forty of the president's longtime friends were gathered. Once more Nixon explained why he had chosen to resign. Then he spoke to them about his wide-ranging concerns, both domestic and foreign, but a flood of tears streaming down his face interrupted his comments. Soon there was not a dry eye in the room. It was only a half hour until the time he would address the American people. Nixon returned to the Oval Office to calm himself and prepare for the telecast.

At nine o'clock in the evening, wearing his usual dark blue suit with an American flag pin in his lapel, he started to read his sixteen-minute speech.

> *From the discussions I have had with Congressional and other leaders, I have concluded that because of the Watergate matter I might not have the support of the Congress that I would consider necessary to back the very difficult decisions and carry out the duties of this office in the way the interests of this nation would require.*
>
> *I have never been a quitter. To leave office before my term is completed is abhorrent to every instinct in my body. But as President, I must put the interest of*

America first. America needs a full-time President and a full-time Congress, particularly at this time with the problems we face at home and abroad. . . .

I regret deeply any injuries that may have been done in the course of the events that led to this decision. I would say only that if some of my judgments were wrong, and some were wrong, they were made in what I believed at the time to be the best interest of the nation. 5

Before he concluded his statement, the president went on to review his achievements in foreign policy and his efforts to bring peace to the nation and the world. Nowhere in the text of his statement did he admit that he was guilty of any crime, any violation of the Constitution. The reason he offered for his resignation was political, not moral: quite simply, he lacked the support he needed to function effectively.

The president rejoined his family for an interval and then met with Chief of Staff Haig to reminisce about his foreign policy achievements. A little while later he phoned his lawyer Leonard Garment to ask what might happen next. Garment could not say. "There are worse things than jail. There is no telephone there. There is, instead, peace. A hard table to write on. The best political writing in this century has been done from jail," the president commented.6 Nixon spent the remainder of the evening on the phone with his congressional supporters discussing his decision not to fight the impeachment charges.

The next morning he signed the resignation letter. After thanking the household staff for their service, the Nixon family walked into the East Room for a final farewell to the assembled Cabinet, White House staff, and friends. Television cameras broadcast his parting words to them. Nixon spoke without a prepared text. He rambled on about his parents' struggles to raise and support their family and how no members of his staff had left the White House richer than when they came in. Quoting Teddy Roosevelt, he spoke about the disappointments people receive in life, the death of loved ones, failure to pass a bar exam, an electoral defeat, but, he counseled, life goes on. "We want you to be proud of what you've done. We want you to continue to serve in government if that is your wish. Always give your best."7 A few minutes later, Richard Nixon and his family left the room full of sobbing people.

Gerald Ford and his wife met with the Nixons to escort them from the White House. The two men exchanged handshakes, and Nixon wished the Fords well. Then the Nixons proceeded to a waiting helicopter and started on the first leg of their trip back to California. Accompanying Richard Nixon on the plane were Defense Department briefcases that contained the country's nuclear strike options. Until Kissinger formally received the resignation letter, Nixon was technically president of the United States. At 11:35, the briefcases became inoperative, and Gerald Ford took over the awesome responsibility for the nation's nuclear response. Officially, Gerald Ford only became president at noon when, in keeping with his request, he was sworn in at a simple inauguration ceremony.

One month later, Sunday, September 8, President Ford went on nationwide television to announce that he was pardoning Richard Nixon for any federal crimes he might have committed in office. The new president explained that either the controversy over Watergate could "go on and on, or someone must write 'The End' to it. I have concluded that only I can do that. And if I can, I must."8 As president, Ford had the power to issue a pardon. Ford's staff had consulted with Leon Jaworski and other experts about the legal problems that might arise were the former president to be brought to trial. This is why Ford was "compelled to conclude that many months and perhaps years will have to pass before Richard Nixon could hope to obtain a fair trial by jury in any jurisdiction of the United States."9 Every newspaper in the country had reported on the details of Nixon's participation in the cover-up. Approximately 92 million Americans had watched the House Judiciary Committee's proceedings on television. If legal procedures had to be delayed indefinitely in the interest of giving the president the right every American has, the right to a fair trial, it would be all the more difficult to heal a divided nation. Ford was also prepared to pardon the former president on humanitarian grounds. He told television viewers, "It is common knowledge that serious allegations and accusations hang like a sword over our former president's head and threaten his health as he tries to reshape his life, a great part of which was spent in service of this country and by the mandate of its people."10

The pardon caused a tremendous uproar. Nixon contributed to the sense of national outrage with the statement he released upon accepting the pardon.

> I know that many fair-minded people believe that my motivation and actions in the Watergate affair were intentionally self-serving and illegal. I now understand how my own mistakes and misjudgments have contributed to that belief and seemed to support it. This burden is the heaviest one of all to bear. That the way I tried to deal with Watergate was the wrong way is a burden I shall bear for every day of the life that is left to me.11

The president was willing to concede that he had made mistakes, but he refused to admit that he was guilty. Of course, accepting the pardon itself was a tacit acknowledgement of guilt. Some felt the president should have been brought to trial. Others disagreed. Many claimed that Nixon had made a deal with Ford. However, there is no evidence that he struck a deal with Gerald Ford as a condition of his resignation. In fact, the former president had expected to go to jail. While intense, the controversy was short-lived since the pardon was irreversible.

What was lost in all the arguments over the pardon was the realization that Richard Nixon had already been punished for his actions. In the words of Gerald Ford in the Proclamation of Pardon, Nixon had "paid the unprecedented penalty of relinquishing the highest office in the United States."[12] Nixon had resigned from the presidency with his reputation in shreds and had had to give his pledge that he would never seek elective office again. For a man who had made politics his life, this was a crushing blow. Perhaps the penalties of the law had not been exacted, but, seen from another perspective, justice was served.

After leaving office under a cloud of accusations, the sixty-one-year-old Nixon took refuge in California. Later he moved to New York and eventually settled in New Jersey. He drew a federal pension and receives all the perquisites of a former president: expense-paid secretarial help, secret service protection, and free offices. He was disbarred from the legal profession, but nevertheless he developed a new career as an author and as the subject of television interviews. Reminiscent of the transition he made once before—after he lost the California governorship—he changed from a bitter, defeated man to an experienced elder statesman. Once more his image was miraculously cleaned up and made acceptable to the American public.

Once the living symbol of a corrupt administration, in

the 1980s he was consulted as a font of wisdom in matters of foreign policy. Not even his worst enemies begrudged the brilliant international moves he made as president. Despite his otherwise checkered career, he reopened relations with China after a mutually hostile twenty-year hiatus and managed to reach an accommodation with the defensive Soviet Union in arms control. His administration also saw the unpopular Vietnam War grind to a halt. This is why government officials still sought his advice.

Almost twenty years after the pardon, Nixon reflected on the Watergate affair in his book *In the Arena: A Memoir of Victory, Defeat, and Renewal.* His memoirs indicate that of the many serious charges hurled against him, he was only willing to concede that he had been too zealous in protecting his subordinates and too lax in setting ethical guidelines.

Unlike the former president, members of the Nixon administration have had their day in court. More than forty members of the government pleaded guilty or were tried for criminal offenses related to the Watergate cover-up, the Ellsberg affair, and campaign irregularities. Included among them were two former cabinet members, twelve members of the White House staff, and fourteen others in the executive branch. Executives of twenty large corporations were penalized for their illegal contributions to Nixon's campaign funds. Of the twenty-five men who went to prison, none served a sentence longer than four and a half years.

Among the major figures in the Watergate scandal, former cabinet official John Mitchell was paroled after nineteen months in prison. He was the only attorney general in the nation's history to be imprisoned. He died in November 1988. Bob Haldeman and John Ehrlichman served eighteen-month sentences and went on to write successful books about their roles in the Watergate affair.

Watergate mastermind Gordon Liddy received the longest sentence, spending fifty-two months in prison. He went on to lecture before college audiences. After thirty-three months in prison, ringleader E. Howard Hunt went back to writing spy novels. John Dean pleaded guilty and received a light four-month sentence in exchange for the information he gave to federal prosecutors. Two minor figures, Jeb Magruder and Charles Colson, both pleaded guilty and were sent to prison for seven months. After their release, they became active in religious causes. Incidentally, another former cabinet officer, Maurice Stans, of slush-fund fame, paid a $5000 fine for violating campaign finance laws.[13]

*   *   *

In the aftermath of the Watergate affair, a mood of reform swept the nation's lawmakers. For them, the House and Senate hearings on the illegal activities of the Nixon administration had proven to be most educational. Outraged by the way the institutions of government had been corrupted for personal gain and power, the legislators were determined to remedy the situation. In 1974, Congress passed the Federal Election Campaign Act. The law set overall ceilings on presidential campaign contributions and spending and tightened campaign finance reporting rules. A novel feature of the act was the provision for limited federal funding of presidential candidates, an effort to reduce the role of private money in elections. Congress also created a Federal Elections Commission to administer the law.

Having taken care of the most obvious offense, Congress enacted other safeguards against wrongdoing. In the same year, the lawmakers strengthened the 1966 Freedom of Information Act, giving citizens access to public records. Under the 1974 act, courts could now review government decisions to withhold national security material from the public, definitions of national security were made more precise, and federal agencies were ordered to act more promptly on requests for information. Then in 1975–1976, the legislators looked into charges of CIA and FBI abuses of power. Such activities as the CIA's involvement in domestic surveillance and the FBI's political use of wiretapping came under fire. Even state governments got into the reform act. Many legislatures passed "sunshine laws," requiring state and local agencies to operate in public, making it possible for citizens to have more information about government decisions.[14]

When the dust settled on this outburst of moralistic fervor, it was business as usual in the American political arena. As the legislators soon found out, laws could place limits on power but they could hardly change human nature. Under the Ford administration, Department of Justice probes revealed that three members of the House of Representatives accepted bribes from Tongsun Park, an Asian rice broker, in what became known as the Koreagate scandal. Congress disciplined three members and cleared eight others. Only one representative went to prison. He pleaded guilty to having defrauded the government.

Despite Jimmy Carter's unquestionable integrity and high moral standards, neither his administration nor the Congress proved immune to the lures of greed. The Democratic president's younger brother Billy was found to have accepted $220,000 from the Libyan government but failed to register as an agent of a foreign government. A Senate inquiry into the "Billygate" scandal revealed Billy had done very little for the Libyans. Republicans complained of a cover-up when it was learned that the attorney general Griffin B. Bell had told the president about his brother's dealings. Then Carter's budget director Bert Lance left office under a cloud. He was accused of financial mis-management of bank funds and other shady dealings when he was president of a Georgia bank. A jury acquitted him of most of the charges. Eventually, he paid a fine and was barred from holding office in any federally insured bank. Then in 1980, it was Congress's turn to be embarrassed. The FBI disclosed the results of its twenty-three-month undercover sting operation in which a phony Arab sheik was videotaped bribing seven susceptible members of Congress. They all went to prison. [15]

Similar scandals involving payoffs and bribery plagued the Reagan administration. However, it was the Iran-Contra affair that captured the headlines and sparked a public furor. Unlike the other scandals, the Iran-Contra affair had more to do with the abuse of power than with greed and corruption. The shadow of Watergate returned to hover over this disclosure of official wrongdoing. Like President Nixon, President Reagan preferred to delegate the responsibilities of governing to subordinates. Like President Nixon, his hands-off approach to government got him into trouble.

Members of Reagan's White House staff stood accused of abusing power, of exceeding their authority. They had secretly sold arms to the Iranians and used the money to fund aid to the Contra rebels fighting in Nicaragua. The arms sale was negotiated in the hope of securing the release of American hostages held by Lebanese Shiite Muslims, thought to be under Iranian control. To get around Congress's Boland Amendment cutting off further American military aid to the Contras, the president's men used the proceeds of their arms sale to supply the Contra rebels fighting the communist Sandinista regime in Nicaragua.

Involved in the complicated maneuvers to sell arms to Iran and convert the cash into military supplies for the Contras was National Security Advisor Robert McFarlane, later replaced by Vice Admiral John Poindexter. Both men worked closely with National Security Council aide Marine Lieutenant Colonel Oliver North, who arranged the actual trades. Other participants in the Iran-Contra affair included retired Air Force General Richard Secord and his partner Albert Hakim, who served as middlemen, and probably CIA Director William Casey, who died during investigations of the affair.

Suspicions of a cover-up began to grow as people reviewed the president's remarks about the affair. On November 13, 1986, President Reagan issued a denial, claiming, "We did not—repeat—we did not trade weapons or anything else for hostages."[16] On February 20, 1987, he stated, "I don't remember—period!"[17] By March 4, President Reagan confessed, "I told the American people I did not trade arms for hostages. My heart and my best intentions still tell me that's true. But the facts and the evidence tell me it is not."[18] Echoes from the past haunted the present as people revised a memorable phrase and asked, "What did the President forget and when did he forget it?"

The president evidently forgot much of what had happened during the Iran-Contra affair, but efforts were made to refresh his memory. The Senate Select Committee on Intelligence and a presidential commission, under John Tower, looked into the matter. Throughout the summer of 1987, specially impanelled committees of the House and Senate held nationally televised joint hearings. Members of Congress heard witnesses testify that they had shredded documents and lied to conceal what they had done.

The major conspirators in the Iran-Contra affair faced legal penalties for their actions. On March 16, 1988, a federal grand jury indicted Oliver North, John Poindexter, Richard Secord, and Albert Hakim. They were accused of a conspiracy to defraud the United States and theft of government property. Five days earlier, Robert McFarlane pleaded guilty to having withheld information from Congress. In the spring of 1989, North's trial, the first to be held, took place. He was sentenced on July 5 to two years of probation, a $150,000 fine, and 1200 hours of community service. The following autumn, Secord and Hakim pleaded guilty to lesser charges as Poindexter awaited trial. In April 1990, Poindexter was convicted for his role in the Iran-Contra cover-up. [19]

It is certainly true that the Iran-Contra affair was not an "instant replay" of the Watergate scandal. However, when the president's men misdirect and distort the instruments of government to accomplish what they believe to be the president's will, whether in foreign policy or domestic politics, the public has every reason to be deeply troubled. When a self-protective president is repeatedly compelled to lie about his actions, the public should feel outraged. In both the Watergate and Iran-Contra affairs, government officials abused the power entrusted to them. They violated the letter and the spirit of the United States Constitution.

When people elect a candidate to the nation's highest office, they have every reason to expect that he and those who carry out his wishes will respect the Constitution. However, the Constitution does not guarantee that the elections will bring to office America's most honorable or capable citizens. America's founders anticipated this. That is why they built a complicated system of rivalries and competition into the framework of the national government. Congress and the courts can put powerful roadblocks in the way of a president who steps out of bounds. As Sam Ervin reasoned, "One of the great advantages of the three separate branches of government is that it's difficult to corrupt all three at the same time."[20] The press corps and television reporters can also act as watchdogs. They serve as the eyes and ears of the American public, prepared to expose wrongdoing in high places.

However, if there is any lesson to be learned from the Watergate break-in and cover-up, it is this. We as Americans must set a climate of opinion and a moral standard that clearly define what we expect of our officeholders. If we are willing to tolerate a break-in at a political party's national committee headquarters and initially regard it as a mere campaign caper or a prank, then we will get what we deserve. Responsibility for the kind of government we get ultimately rests with us.

WHO'S WHO
IN THE
WATERGATE CRISIS

The Watergate Burglars

Ringleaders
  Howard Hunt
  G. Gordon Liddy
Burglars
  Bernard Barker
  Virgilio Gonzalez
  Eugenio Martinez
  James McCord, Jr.
  Frank Sturgis

Committee to Reelect the President

  Herbert Kalmbach, Deputy
    Finance Chairman
  Frederick La Rue, Deputy
    Director
  Jeb Stuart Magruder, Deputy
    Director
  John Mitchell, Director
  Maurice Stans, Finance
    Chairman

White House Staff

  Alexander Butterfield, Deputy
    Assistant to the President

Charles Colson, Special
    Counsel
John Dean, Special Counsel
John Ehrlichman, Assistant to
    the President for Domestic
    Affairs
Alexander Haig, Chief of Staff
H. R. Haldeman, Chief of Staff
Henry Kissinger, Assistant to
    the President for National
    Security Affairs
Rose Mary Woods, secretary
Ronald Ziegler, Press Secretary
The President's Attorneys
    J. Frederick Buzhardt
    Leonard Garment
    James D. St. Clair

Cabinet Members and Subordinates

Robert Bork, Solicitor General
Archibald Cox, Special
    Prosecutor
L. Patrick Gray, Acting
    Director of the FBI
Leon Jaworski, Special
    Prosecutor

Henry Kissinger, Secretary of
State
Richard Kleindienst, Attorney
General
John Mitchell, Attorney
General
Henry Petersen, Assistant
Attorney General
Elliot Richardson, Attorney
General
William Saxbe, Attorney
General
Vernon Walters, Deputy
Director of the Central
Intelligence Agency

Congress

Senate
Howard Baker, Vice
Chairman of the
Watergate Committee
Samuel Dash, Staff Director
of the Watergate
Committee
Sam Ervin, Chairman of the
Watergate Committee
Barry Goldwater, Senator
from Arizona
House of Representatives
John Doar, Chief Counsel to
the House Judiciary
Committee
Wright Patman, Chairman of
the Committee on
Banking and Currency
Peter Rodino, Chairman of
the House Judiciary
Committee

Charles Wiggins, member of
the House Judiciary
Committee

Reporters

Carl Bernstein, the *Washington
Post*
Seymour Hersh, the *New York
Times*
Daniel Schorr, CBS News
Bob Woodward, the *Washington
Post*

Judges

Warren Burger, Chief Justice of
the Supreme Court
John Sirica, Chief Judge, U.S.
District Court for the District
of Columbia

Vice Presidents of the United States

Spiro T. Agnew
Gerald R. Ford

Others

Daniel Ellsberg, defense analyst
George McGovern, 1972
Democratic presidential
candidate

HIGHLIGHTS OF
THE WATERGATE SCANDAL

1972

June 17—Five men are arrested during an attempted break-in at Democratic Party Headquarters.

June 20—The president discusses the break-in with John Mitchell and then with Bob Haldeman. The tape of this conversation was missing because of an 18½-minute gap.

June 22—In his first public comment on the break-in, President Nixon denies White House involvement in the incident at a press conference.

June 23—The president and Haldeman arrange to thwart the FBI's investigation of the attempted burglary.

July 1—John Mitchell resigns as manager of President Nixon's reelection campaign.

August 29—At a presidential press conference Nixon defends his aides from charges of mishandling campaign funds and states that John Dean's investigation of the White House staff revealed no connection with the burglary.

September 15—Federal grand jury indictments are issued against Watergate burglars. The president praises John Dean for handling the cover-up so successfully.

November 7—Richard Nixon is reelected president.

1973

January 8–30—The trial of Watergate burglars before Judge John Sirica is held.

February 7—The Senate votes 77–0 to set up a select committee to investigate charges of corruption in the 1972 elections.

February 27—John Dean discusses the cover-up with the president.

March 23—James McCord confesses to perjury and admits that politicians had approved plans for the burglary.

April 30—Nixon announces that John Ehrlichman, Bob Haldeman, John Dean, and Richard Kleindienst have resigned.

May 17—The Senate Select Committee on Presidential Campaign Activities, Sam Ervin's Watergate Committee, begins public hearings on Watergate.

May 18—Archibald Cox is appointed special prosecutor.

May 22—The president denies that he knew about the Watergate break-in but admits that he limited the scope of the investigation in the interest of national security.

June 25–29—Dean testifies before the Ervin committee and accuses the president of a cover-up.

July 13—Alexander Butterfield tells the staff of the Watergate Committee about the existence of presidential tapes.

August 29—Judge Sirica rules the president must turn over subpoenaed tapes to the special prosecutor, and Nixon appeals the decision.

October 10—Vice President Spiro T. Agnew resigns.

October 12—The Court of Appeals orders Nixon to surrender the Watergate tapes. Gerald Ford is nominated as vice president.

October 20—Nixon's Saturday Night Massacre results in the resignations of Elliot Richardson and William Ruckelshaus. Robert Bork fires Cox.

October 23—Announcement is made that subpoenaed tapes will be turned over to Judge Sirica.

November 1—Leon Jaworski is named special prosecutor.

November 17—President Nixon declares at a news conference that he is not a crook.

November 21—The existence of an $18\frac{1}{2}$-minute gap in the tapes is made public.

1974

February 6—The House of Representatives votes to start impeachment proceedings against the president and gives the Judiciary Committee broad subpoena power.

March 1—A federal grand jury indicts John Mitchell, Bob Haldeman, John Ehrlichman, Charles Colson, and three others. Nixon is named as an unindicted coconspirator.

April 11—The Judiciary Committee subpoenas forty-two tapes.

April 29—Nixon announces on television that he is voluntarily releasing 1,200 pages of edited transcripts of the tapes to the Judiciary Committee.

May 24—Jaworski appeals directly to the Supreme Court for a ruling on his subpoena for sixty-four tapes.

July 24—The Supreme Court rules 8–0 in *United States* v. *Nixon* that the president must turn over the tapes.

July 27–30—The House Judiciary Committee votes three articles of impeachment.

July 29—The presidential tapes, revealing that on June 23, 1972, Nixon had ordered Haldeman to block the FBI investigation of Watergate, are turned over to Judge Sirica and the Congress.

August 5—Senator Barry Goldwater and two other high-ranking Republican senators tell Nixon that he can count on no more than fifteen votes in the Senate.

August 9—President Nixon resigns and Gerald Ford becomes president.

September 8—President Gerald Ford pardons Richard Nixon.

ACKNOWLEDGMENTS

I would like to thank the following people for helping me with this book: Jess Bunshaft for clarifying legal concepts, Marilyn Bunshaft for locating certain descriptive materials, Suzanne Freedman for assisting me with some of the research, and Reni Roxas, my editor at Franklin Watts, for proposing the topic to me and making a number of useful suggestions. I am indebted to my teenage son Doug for pointing out sections of the manuscript that needed to be made more exciting. I am especially grateful to my husband, Gerald Feinberg, for all that he did to make it possible for me to write this book.

PHOTOGRAPHY CREDITS

All photographs courtesy of UPI/Bettmann Newsphotos
except: Photo Researchers: insert p. 1 bottom (Don Carl Steffen);
Rothco Cartoons: insert p. 12 top (von Hedemann).

NOTES

Chapter One
A Third-Rate Burglary Attempt

1 Theodore H. White, *Breach of Faith: The Fall of Richard Nixon* (New York: Atheneum, 1975), 141.

2 White, 154.

3 White, 161.

4 "Nixon, Bitter at his Defeat by Brown in California, Denounces Press as Biased," *New York Times*, 8 November 1962, 18.

5 Quoted in Henry Kissinger, *Years of Upheaval* (Boston: Little Brown & Co., 1982), 77; Jonathan Schell, *The Time of Illusion* (New York: Vintage Books, 1976), 265; Bob Woodward and Carl Bernstein, *All the President's Men* (New York: Warner Books, 1975), 26.

6 "Transcript of the President's News Conference Emphasizing Domestic Matters," *New York Times*, 23 June 1972, 18.

7 Woodward and Bernstein, 19.

Chapter Two
The Slush Fund

1 Much of the material in this chapter summarizes incidents described in Bob Woodward and Carl Bernstein, *All the President's Men* (New York: Warner Books, 1975). For a complete account of the two reporters' investigation of the Watergate scandal, readers are urged to consult their book.

2 Woodward and Bernstein, 73–74.

3 Woodward and Bernstein, 74.

4 Mentioned in Woodward and Bernstein, 30, but the details are provided in Jonathan Schell, *The Time of Illusion* (New York: Vintage Books, 1976), 240.

5   "Transcript of News Conference by the President on Political and Other Matters," *New York Times*, 30 August 1972, 20.

6   "Transcript," 20.

7   John Dean, *Blind Ambition* (New York: Pocket Books, 1977), 129.

8   Quoted material between Judge Sirica and the Watergate defendants found in Woodward and Bernstein, 260–261, and partially in Schell, 305.

9   Woodward and Bernstein, 268.

Chapter Three
Stonewalling It

1   John Dean, *Blind Ambition* (New York: Pocket Books, 1977), 19.

2   Dean, 116.

3   Leon Jaworski, *The Right and the Power* (Houston: Gulf Publishing Company, 1976), 213–214; The Staff of the *Washington Post*, "The Complete Transcript of the New Tapes [June 23, 1972]," *The Fall of a President*, (New York: Dell Books, 1974), 209–210.

4   Jaworski, 212; "The Complete Transcript of the New Tapes [June 23, 1972]," 208.

5   Jaworski, 214; "The Complete Transcript of the New Tapes [June 23, 1972]," 215.

6   "Meeting: The President, Haldeman, and Dean, Oval Office, September 15, 1972," *The Presidential Transcripts* (New York: Dell Books, 1974), 32.

7   "Meeting: The President, Haldeman, and Dean, Oval Office, September 15, 1972," 34.

8   "Meeting: The President, Haldeman, and Dean, Oval Office, September 15, 1972," 34.

9   "Meeting: The President, Haldeman, and Dean, Oval Office, September 15, 1972," 36.

10   "Meeting: The President, Haldeman, and Dean, Oval Office, September 15, 1972," 37–38.

11   "Meeting: The President, Haldeman, and Dean, Oval Office, September 15, 1972," 40.

Chapter Four
A Cap on the Bottle

1   "Meeting: The President and Dean, Oval Office, February 29, 1973," *The Presidential Transcripts* (New York: Dell Books, 1974), 59.

2   "Meeting: The President and Dean, Oval Office, February 29, 1973," 59.

[3] "Meeting: The President and Dean, Oval Office, March 13, 1973," *The Presidential Transcripts* (New York: Dell Books, 1974), 70.

[4] "Meeting: The President and Dean, Oval Office, March 13, 1973," 75.

[5] "Meeting: The President, Dean, and Haldeman, Oval Office, March 21, 1973," *The Presidential Transcripts* (New York: Dell Books, 1974), 99.

[6] "Meeting: The President, Dean, and Haldeman, Oval Office, March 21, 1973," 110.

[7] "Meeting: The President, Dean, and Haldeman, Oval Office, March 21, 1973," 112.

[8] "Meeting: The President, Dean, and Haldeman, Oval Office, March 21, 1973," 115–116.

[9] "Meeting: The President, Dean, and Haldeman, Oval Office, March 21, 1973," 145.

[10] "Meeting: The President, Dean, and Haldeman, Oval Office, March 21, 1973," 145.

[11] "Remarks by Principals in Watergate Sentencings," *New York Times*, 24 March 1973, 12.

[12] Theodore H. White, *Breach of Faith: The Fall of Richard Nixon* (New York: Atheneum, 1975), 205.

[13] "Meeting: The President, Haldeman, Ehrlichman, and Ziegler, Oval Office, March 27, 1973," *The Presidential Transcripts* (New York: Dell Books, 1974), 197.

[14] White, 209.

[15] "Meeting: The President, Haldeman, and Ehrlichman, Oval Office, April 14, 1973," *The Presidential Transcripts* (New York: Dell Books, 1974), 242.

[16] "Statement: The President, April 17, 1973," *The Presidential Transcripts* (New York: Dell Books, 1974), 606–607.

[17] "Meeting: The President, Petersen, and Ziegler, Oval Office, April 27, 1973, *The Presidential Transcripts* (New York: Dell Books, 1974), 675.

[18] "Statement: The President, April 30, 1973," *The Presidential Transcripts* (New York: Dell Books, 1974), 687.

[19] "Statement: The President, April 30, 1973," 687.

Chapter Five
The Saturday Night Massacre

[1] Bob Woodward and Carl Bernstein, *All the President's Men* (New York: Warner Books, 1975), 275.

[2] "Text of Statement by Nixon," *New York Times*, 23 May 1973, 28.

3   "Text of Statement by Nixon," 28.
4   Theodore H. White, *Breach of Faith: The Fall of Richard Nixon* (New York: Atheneum, 1975), 235.
5   White, 236. See dialogues between the president and his aides in Chapters 3 and 4 for excerpts from the tapes.
6   Bob Woodward and Carl Bernstein, *The Final Days* (New York: Avon Books, 1976), 97.
7   White, 153.
8   The actual A.C. Nielsen ratings for specific daytime television programs compared with the televised Watergate hearings are listed in Ben H. Bagdikian, "Newspapers Learning (Too Slowly) to Adapt to TV," *Watergate and the Political Process*, ed. Ronald E. Pynn (New York: Praeger Publishers, 1975), 84.
9   White, 240.
10 "Excerpts from the Transcript of Cox's News Conference on Nixon's Decision on Tapes," *New York Times*, 21 October 1973, 60.
11 "Transcript of Nixon's Question and Answer Session with A. P. Managing Editors," *New York Times*, 18 November 1973, 62.

Chapter Six
The Smoking Gun

1   Theodore H. White, *Breach of Faith: The Fall of Richard Nixon* (New York: Atheneum, 1975), 278.
2   "Transcript of Nixon's Address to the Nation Regarding Controversy over Tapes," *New York Times*, 30 April 1974, 32.
3   "Transcript of Nixon's Address," 32.
4   "Transcript of Nixon's Address," 32.
5   Bob Woodward and Carl Bernstein, *The Final Days* (New York: Avon Books, 1976), 149. See Chapters 3 and 4 for excerpts from the tapes.
6   White, 298.
7   Leon Jaworski, *The Right and the Power* (Houston: Gulf Publishing Company, 1976), 191.
8   Woodward and Bernstein, 273.
9   Woodward and Bernstein, 276.
10 *United States v. Nixon* 418 U.S. 683 (1974), reprinted in Ronald E. Pym, ed., *Watergate and the American Political Process* (New York: Praeger Publishers, 1975), 236–246.
11 White, 314.
12 Jaworski, 210; "President's Statement about Disclosure," *New York Times*, 6 August 1974, 1. See Chapter 3 for excerpts from the June 23 tapes.
13 "From the Minority Report," *World Almanac 1975* (New York: Newspaper Enterprise Association, 1974), 39–40.

Chapter Seven
The End to It

1   Henry Kissinger, *Years of Upheaval* (Boston: Little Brown & Co., 1982), 1205; also see Kissinger, p. 1197, for an evaluation of Haig's contribution to the last days of the Nixon presidency; for a more detailed discussion of Haig's actions, see Bob Woodward and Carl Bernstein, *The Final Days* (New York: Avon Books, 1976), 391, 425, 442–443, 447–448, 450, 453–455, 460, 464, 474, 478, 479–480, 484, 499, 504.

2   Woodward and Bernstein, 461.

3   For two different versions of the meeting between the president and his secretary of state, see Kissinger, 1207–1210, and Woodward and Bernstein, 469–472.

4   Woodward and Bernstein, 491.

5   "Transcript of President Nixon's Address to the Nation Announcing his Resignation," *New York Times*, 9 August 1974, 2.

6   Woodward and Bernstein, 501.

7   "Transcript of Nixon's Farewell Speech to Cabinet and Staff Members in the Capital," *New York Times*, 10 August 1974, 4.

8   "Statement by the President in Connection with His Proclamation Pardoning Nixon," *New York Times*, 9 September 1974, 24.

9   "Statement by the President," 24.

10 "Statement by the President," 24.

11 "The Statement by Nixon," *New York Times*, 9 September 1974, 1.

12 "Proclamation of Pardon," *New York Times*, 9 September 1974, 1.

13 For a more thorough account of the penalties paid by participants in the Watergate scandal, see John Blum, Edmund Morgan, Willie Lee Rose, Arthur M. Schlesinger, Jr., Kenneth Stamp, and C. Vann Woodward, *The National Experience*, 5th ed. (New York: Harcourt Brace Jovanovich, 1981), 863 & 865; Leon Jaworski, *The Right and the Power* (Houston: Gulf Publishing Company, 1976), 280–292; Shelley Ross, *Fall from Grace* (New York: Ballantine Books, 1988), 230–232; "Where Are They Now," *Newsweek*, 14 June 1982, 42 and 45.

14 Watergate reforms developed from John Blum and others, 856–866; James McGregor Burns, J. W. Peltason, and Thomas E. Cronin, *Government by the People*, 9th ed. (Englewood Cliffs, N.J.: Prentice-Hall, Inc, 1975), 145, 331; Ross, 233–234.

15 A more detailed discussion of scandals during the Ford and Carter years can be found in Ross, 235–268.

16 Bernard Weinraub, "Reagan Confirms Iran Got Arms Aid," *New York Times*, 13 November 1986, 1.

17 "Panel Said to Hear of Effort to Hide Reagan Iran Role," *New York Times*, 20 February 1987, 1.

[18] "Transcript of Reagan's Speech: 'I Take Full Responsibility for My Actions,'" *New York Times*, 5 March 1987, 18.

[19] Ross, 279–80; "Ollie Learns His Fate," *Time*, 17 July 1989, 65; Frances Fitzgerald, "Annals of Justice: Iran-Contra," *The New Yorker*, 16 October 1989, 84; "Secord Makes a Deal," *Time*, 20 November 1989, 69; "And Then There Was One," *Time*, 4 December 1989, 49; "Poindexter is Found Guilty of All Five Criminal Charges for Iran–Contra Cover-Up," *New York Times*. 8 April 1990, 1.

[20] Blum and others, 865.

BIBLIOGRAPHY

"And Then There Was One," *Time*, 4 December 1989, 49.

Blum, John, Edmund Morgan, Willie Lee Rose, Arthur M. Schlesinger, Jr., Kenneth Stamp, and C. Vann Woodward. *The National Experience*, 5th ed. New York: Harcourt Brace Jovanovich, 1981, pp. 842–866.

Burns, James MacGregor, J. W. Peltason, and Thomas E. Cronin. *Government by the People*, 9th ed. Englewood Cliffs, N.J.: Prentice-Hall, Inc., 1975.

Dean, John. *Blind Ambition*. New York: Pocket Books, 1977.

Fitzgerald, Frances. "Annals of Justice: Iran-Contra," *The New Yorker*, 16 October 1989, 51–84.

Jaworski, Leon. *The Right and the Power*. Houston: Gulf Publishing Company, 1976.

Kissinger, Henry. *Years of Upheaval*. Boston: Little Brown and Co., 1982.

New York Times.

Nixon, Richard. *In the Arena: A Memoir of Victory, Defeat, and Renewal*. New York: Simon and Shuster, 1990.

"Ollie Learns His Fate," *Time*, 17 July 1989, 65.

Pynn, Ronald E., ed. *Watergate and the American Political Process*. New York: Praeger Publishers, 1975.

Ross, Shelley. *Fall from Grace: Sex, Scandal and Corruption in American Politics from 1702 to the Present.* New York: Ballantine Books, 1988.

Schell, Jonathan. *The Time of Illusion.* New York: Vintage Books, 1976.

"Secord Makes a Deal," *Time*, 20 November 1989, 69.

The Presidential Transcripts. New York: Dell Books, 1974.

The Staff of the *Washington Post. The Fall of a President.* New York: Dell Books, 1974.

"Where Are They Now," *Newsweek.* 14 June 1982, 42 and 45.

White, Theodore H. *Breach of Faith: The Fall of Richard Nixon.* New York: Atheneum, 1975.

Woodward, Bob, and Carl Bernstein. *All the President's Men.* New York: Warner Books, 1975.

_____. *The Final Days.* New York: Avon Books, 1976.

The World Almanac. New York: Newspaper Enterprise Association, 1974–1976, 1988–1989.

INDEX

House of Representatives, 88, 101, 102, 104, 105
Humphrey, Hubert H., 24
Hunt, E. Howard, *insert* 3, 20, 21, 24, 28, 29–30, 33, 34, 35–38, 42, 58, 74, 92, 98–99, 115

Immunity, 65
Impeachment, *insert* 12, 83, 85, 88, 89–90, 94–104, 107, 109
Inouye, Daniel, 70
Internal Revenue Service, 76
Iran-Contra affair, 117–119

Jaworski, Leon, *insert* 11, 83–85, 87, 90–91, 93, 95–98, 111
Johnson, Andrew, 90
Johnson, Lyndon B., 47, 73, 78, 89
Justice Department, 32, 33, 45, 49–50, 66, 71, 80, 88, 116

Kelley, Clarence B., 56
Kennedy, John F., 23, 73, 78, 89
Kennedy, Ted, 29, 50
Khrushchev, Nikita, 23
Kissinger, Henry, *insert* 14, 76, 106, 107, 108, 111
Kleindienst, Richard, *insert* 5, 21, 33–34, 63, 66, 67

LaRue, Frederick C., 20–21
Liddy, G. Gordon, *insert* 3, 20, 21, 24, 30–31, 34, 57, 115; Watergate trial and sentencing, 33, 35–38, 43

Magruder, Jeb Stuart, 20–21, 57, 115; testimony of, 62, 63, 72
Martinez, Eugenio, *insert* 3, 17, 36, 37
McCord, James W., Jr., *insert* 3, 17, 21, 25, 27, 29, 37, 60–61, 71
McGovern, George, 34, 89

Milk Fund disclosure, 76
Mitchell, John, 20, 21, 25, 30, 32, 36, 43, 44, 57, 58, 66, 72, 83, 92, 96, 97, 114; resignation of, 25; as Watergate scapegoat, 61–62
Montoya, Joseph, 70

New York Times, 17, 30, 31, 36
Nixon, Richard M., *insert* 1, *insert* 5, *insert* 10, *insert* 12, *inserts* 14–16; childhood of, 22; cover-up actions of, 41–52, 53–68, 70–88, 90–104; denial of guilt by, 25, 32–33, 45, 64–65, 66–67, 72, 81, 85, 93–94, 103–104, 110, 112–113; early career of, 22–24; on foreign affairs, 23, 34, 79, 97, 110, 114; life after Watergate, 113–114; presidential campaigns of, 23, 24, 25, 34, 47, 51, 57, 77; pardoned by Ford, 111–113; personality of, 17; resignation of, 16, 105–111; and Saturday Night Massacre, 82–83, 87; and Watergate tapes, 78–88, 90–98, 100–104
Nixon family, *insert* 1, *insert* 5, 22, 107

Oval Office, *insert* 1, 93, 107, 109; cover-up sessions, 41–50, 53–66, 73

Patman, Wright, 50, 51
Pentagon Papers, The, 19, 71
Petersen, Henry, 65
Plumbers unit, 18–19, 20, 30, 34–35, 42, 69, 71, 76
Powell, Chief Justice, 101
Presidential elections, 34; 1960, 23, 24, 77; 1968, 24, 47; 1972, 24, 25, 34, 51, 57

★ 144 ★